PUFFIN
APOSTLE

Born in 1974 in Delhi, Rukmini Chawla did a Masters' degree in English Literature at St. Stephen's College, Delhi, and another in Women's Studies at the University of Oxford.

Rukmini has worked in television and currently publishes a magazine called *The Dance of Life*. She has been associated with Mother Teresa and the Missionaries of Charity since childhood.

Rukmini is married and lives in Delhi.

APOSTLE OF LOVE

THE LIFE OF MOTHER TERESA

Rukmini Chawla

PUFFIN BOOKS

PUFFIN BOOKS
Published by the Penguin Group
Penguin Books India Pvt. Ltd, 11 Community Centre, Panchsheel Park, New Delhi 110 017, India
Penguin Group (USA) Inc., 375 Hudson Street, New York, New York 10014, USA
Penguin Group (Canada), 90 Eglinton Avenue East, Suite 700, Toronto, Ontario, M4P 2Y3, Canada (a division of Pearson Penguin Canada Inc.)
Penguin Books Ltd, 80 Strand, London WC2R 0RL, England
Penguin Ireland, 25 St Stephen's Green, Dublin 2, Ireland (a division of Penguin Books Ltd)
Penguin Group (Australia), 250 Camberwell Road, Camberwell, Victoria 3124, Australia (a division of Pearson Australia Group Pty Ltd)
Penguin Group (NZ), cnr Airborne and Rosedale Roads, Albany, Auckland 1310, New Zealand (a division of Pearson New Zealand Ltd)
Penguin Group (South Africa) (Pty) Ltd, 24 Sturdee Avenue, Rosebank, Johannesburg 2196, South Africa

Penguin Books Ltd, Registered Offices: 80 Strand, London WC2R 0RL, England

First published in Puffin by Penguin Books India 2005

Text copyright © Rukmini Chawla 2005
Copyright in the inside illustrations rests with the individual artists

Names of some persons in the text have been changed to protect their identity

All rights reserved

10 9 8 7 6 5 4 3 2 1

ISBN-10: 0143 335162 ISBN-13: 9780143335160

Typeset in Palatino by Mantra Virtual Services, New Delhi
Printed at Pauls Press, New Delhi

This book is sold subject to the condition that it shall not, by way of trade or otherwise, be lent, resold, hired out, or otherwise circulated without the publisher's prior written consent in any form of binding or cover other than that in which it is published and without a similar condition including this condition being imposed on the subsequent purchaser and without limiting the rights under copyright reserved above, no part of this publication may be reproduced, stored in or introduced into a retrieval system, or transmitted in any form or by any means (electronic, mechanical, photocopying, recording or otherwise), without the prior written permission of both the copyright owner and the above-mentioned publisher of this book.

CONTENTS

Dear Rukmini

you

God bless you
Mc Teresa mc

See! I will not forget you ... I have carved
you on the palm of My hand ... I have
called you by your name ... You are mine
... You are precious to Me ... I love you.

Isaiah

Prologue

It is a hot, dusty summer day in Delhi in 1995. I take a left turn at the traffic light on the Mathura road, and drive down a bumpy lane till I reach the grey double-storeyed building at the end of it. Getting out of my car, I find myself standing in front of a large iron gate.

I try to push it, but it is locked. I call out, wondering if someone will hear me. But there is no sign of anyone.

I try banging on the gate and hurt my fist instead. No one comes to open the gate. In one part of my mind, I see this lack of response as a good sign. I am very nervous at the prospect of entering the building. Maybe I am not meant to go in, after all. Maybe I should get back into my car and go home instead.

Just as I turn to leave, I hear footsteps. Someone has heard me.

The gate opens and a *chowkidar* beckons. He leads me to the entrance of the building and into the 'parlour', a small waiting room.

I am in Jeevan Jyoti, Mother Teresa's Home for children. The chowkidar goes to fetch one of the Sisters. I know this is my last chance to leave. Almost without realizing it, I move towards the door—and nearly bang into the Sister who is just stepping in.

You may wonder why I am so reluctant to be here at Jeevan Jyoti. There is a long story behind this, the story of an extraordinary person who has changed the lives of millions around the world. A story so inspiring that I want to be a part of it, yet now, at the last moment, I wonder if I am strong enough.

I have come as a volunteer to spend time with the children at Jeevan Jyoti. All these children have been abandoned by their families who didn't want them, or couldn't keep them. I have no idea what to say to these children. I have all the things they can only dream about: loving parents, a warm, wonderful home, and everything my heart desires. I find myself feeling guilty and embarrassed.

I also wonder what these children will be like. I'm convinced they will be very sad and lonely; what light can there possibly be in their lives? What will I talk to them about?

With a start I realize that the Sister is talking to me. She introduces herself as Sister Ann Vinita. She is warm and friendly as she asks me about my family. Then she says, 'Come, let me take you to see the children; it's their play time.'

She leads me down the corridor. Through the double grill doors, I see a large courtyard. There are about thirty children of various ages running around, shouting and laughing.

As I walk out with her, the children catch sight of me. Their voices die down; there is complete silence. This is even worse than I imagined! I wonder what I should do next. Here I am, I think wryly, an adult, and totally tongue-tied in the presence of these children.

Suddenly, a child of about four or five comes hurtling towards me. He flings himself into my arms, laughing. Before I can understand what is happening, I am surrounded by a whole group of children, all talking excitedly, pulling me in different directions, wanting to play or show me their swings, wanting piggyback rides . . .

Soon I am very busy, with no more time to worry about what

to do with these children. As you can see, they're perfectly capable of taking care of me!

Jeevan Jyoti is only one of the hundreds of Homes for poor children, men and women set up all over India and abroad. One single woman set up all these Homes—houses where countless poor people are given shelter and taken care of. Her name was Mother Teresa and the organization through which she did her work is the Missionaries of Charity.

People around the world become famous for different reasons. There are prime ministers, presidents, kings, queens, actors, writers, musicians, painters, scientists—the list is endless. Despite their fame, they are not always loved. Only on rare occasions you come across someone who is not just well known but is also loved and revered. Mother Teresa was such a person.

Mother Teresa dedicated her life to serving the poor. She lived amongst the poorest of the poor, in the slums and on the streets. Her work was inspired by her love for the poor and suffering people of the world. This book is the incredible story of how a poor, simple nun became one of the most beloved and famous figures of all times.

Mother Teresa helped the poor in all kinds of ways. For children as well as for old, sick, dying and handicapped people, and others who were not able to take care of themselves, Mother Teresa set up special Homes where such people could live and be taken care of. She gave free medical help and started medical centres in India and abroad where poor people with different diseases and health problems could be treated. She also established schools where poor children could be educated.

The most important things that Mother Teresa gave poor people were her love, compassion and understanding She understood that though people need food, clothing and medicines, they need love and support much more. More than physical suffering, it is the feeling of being unwanted and unloved that makes life unbearable. Mother Teresa gave the poor and destitute her love and made them understand that they too were special, that they too were God's children and He loved everyone equally. Her goal was to give them self-confidence and dignity.

Mother Teresa died on 5 September 1997. But the Missionaries of Charity Sisters and Brothers continue working in the way that Mother Teresa had taught them. Every single day, they reach out and help the poorest of the poor in countries all over the world.

My association with Mother Teresa goes back to when I was two years old. My father had become acquainted with her about a year before that.

He was an Indian Administrative Service officer, and Mother Teresa and he met in the course of his work. Over the years, he became closely associated with her and her organization. As her work expanded, she would run into administrative problems every now and then. My father would help her whenever possible to sort out such problems. This association continued till the end of her life.

My earliest memory of Mother Teresa is when she came to our house accompanied by some of her Sisters. It was a very special day for the whole family. Over the years, I had the good fortune of occasionally meeting Mother Teresa when she came to Delhi. Sometimes she even spared a few minutes of her time to come to our house.

There was one thing I noticed as a child: unlike our other guests, Mother Teresa and her Sisters never had anything to eat or drink at our house. Later I learnt that this was a rule that all the Sisters followed. The reason was that when they went to visit the homes of the poor, the people would lovingly offer whatever they had to Mother Teresa and her Sisters, though this sometimes meant that later they would have to go hungry themselves. When Mother Teresa realized this, she decided that she would never eat in other people's homes—not even where there was no shortage of food, as it was not right to discriminate.

When Mother Teresa was in Delhi, my father would visit her wherever in the city she happened to be working. Sometimes he would take me along. When I was in my teens, Mother Teresa suggested that I work as a volunteer in one of her Homes. At that time, working in the Homes was far from my mind. I was preoccupied with my studies and friends. Over the next few years, she mentioned this to me several times, suggesting that I come to Calcutta during school holidays to work with her. But it was only much later, when I was in my twenties, that I began to visit the Homes in Delhi. To my regret, I never visited Calcutta for more than a few days while she was alive.

From childhood, Mother Teresa and her work had a deep impact upon me, and she will always be a source of inspiration. I am deeply grateful that I have been touched by her love and have received her blessings. The Sisters, including many of whom I have had the opportunity to interact with over the years, and the Homes are all very close to my heart. Whenever I visit them, I feel at home. Though it has been several years since Mother Teresa has gone, it does not feel like she has left us at all.

LIFE IN SKOPJE

When Agnes Gonxha Bojaxhiu was born on 26 August 1910, in Üsküb (present-day Skopje), it was a small town in Albania. However, its turbulent political history would see it become a part of Serbia three years later. In 1945, it became the capital of the Yugoslav republic of Macedonia.

Agnes's father Nicholas Bojaxhiu was a prosperous building contractor. He was a kind, well-educated man. He was popular with his friends, and their house was always full of visitors. Her mother Dranafile Bernai was a stern disciplinarian but also very loving. Agnes was the youngest child in the family. Her sister Age was six years older, and her brother Lazar three years older. They were all very close. They lived in a big, comfortable house.

Though the people of Albania were predominantly Muslim, the Bojaxhiu family was Catholic, members of a branch of the Christian Church that regards the Pope at the Vatican in Rome as its spiritual head. There are two other main branches of Christianity: Protestantism and Eastern Orthodoxy. This is just like the different branches in Hinduism, such as the Shaivities and the Vaishnavs, or in Islam, such as Shia and Sunni.

Drana was a very religious woman. She spent a lot of time helping poor people. Nobody who came to her door for help, be it for food or money, was ever turned away. Drana also regularly visited the poor, taking them food and money. Agnes used to accompany her mother on these visits. Years later, she said of her mother, 'She taught us to love God and our neighbour.'

Drana also spent a lot of time in church, and here too, Agnes used to go with her. Mother and daughter would pray together.

Agnes was a serious child. She was neat, helpful and obedient. When her brother Lazar stole into the kitchen late at night to eat sweets, a forbidden act, little Agnes never reported this to her mother. She was studious, and loved to read. The local library was a favourite place to visit. Along with her siblings, she attended the school at the Sacred Heart Church.

Agnes grew up in a secure family, full of love. However busy she was all day with her various tasks, Drana would always be waiting to greet her husband with a smile when he came home from work. As children, Agnes and her siblings used to tease their mother. Later, Agnes understood the tremendous love her mother had for her father. Every evening, the family would pray together and spend time with one another.

When Agnes was seven years old, her father died suddenly. Drana was heartbroken. Matters became worse when Nicholas's partner took over his share of the business and all the money there was in it. The Bojaxhiu family was left penniless. Drana was traumatized, and initially, found it hard to cope with her grief. She leaned on her children for support, especially Age.

It took Drana several months to recover, but she was a brave woman and knew that life had to carry on. She had to find a way to look after her children and herself. She started an embroidery business. After a while, the business began to do very well. Drana made sure that she earned enough so that her children were not lacking in anything.

After Nicholas's death, Age and Agnes began to spend more time in church. They began to participate in the activities of the parish or church community. When Agnes was twelve, she first felt the desire to become a nun and devote her life to the worship and service of God. When she told her mother about this, Drana did not take her very seriously since she was still so young.

It was during this time that Agnes met Father Jambrenkovic, who took a keen interest in the welfare of the young people in his parish. Father Jambrenkovic introduced the sisters to the Sodality of the Blessed Virgin Mary. A sodality is an organization approved by Church authorities and set up for doing works of piety and charity. There are many sodalities dedicated to Mary, which have been in existence since the sixteenth century, and these are found in different communities all over the world. This Sodality had a deep impact on young Agnes, as its central belief was that helping the poor and needy was one of the ways of reaching out to God.

Another activity of the Sodality was to make young people aware of the lives of saints and missionaries. This is how Agnes heard of the priests who went from her country to a faraway land called Bengal, in India, in 1924. Father Jambrenkovic shared the exciting stories of these missionaries with members of the Sodality—about their experiences of working with poor people in Bengal, especially the children. The young people of Skopje prayed for the welfare of the workers in a new country so far away. Agnes was fascinated by the stories of this mysterious land and inspired by the work that the missionaries did.

While still in her teens, Agnes began to teach the children of the community about the Catholic religion. She enjoyed teaching, and she loved children, so this was an ideal occupation for her. She would also teach her classmates whenever they needed help with their school work.

As Agnes's eighteenth birthday drew near, her desire to devote her life to God came back with renewed force. She felt that this was God's will, that God wanted her to dedicate her life to Him by becoming a nun and working with poor people. Many years later, in Calcutta, she spoke of this time in her life: 'At eighteen, I decided to leave home and become a nun. By then I realized that my vocation was towards the poor. From then on, I have never had the least doubt of my decision.' Pointing a finger towards Heaven, she added, 'He made the choice.'

Agnes had been unable to forget the stories she had heard about the missionaries serving the poor in Bengal, and she decided that that was where she wanted to work. She knew this meant leaving her home and family, but she was ready for this.

When Agnes told Drana about this decision, her mother's support was complete. She told her, 'Put your hand in His hand and walk all the way with Him.'

As the first stage, Agnes tried to find out if there were any nuns living in Bengal. She wrote to some of the missionaries in Bengal, who wrote back and informed her that there were indeed nuns there, called the Sisters of Loreto. They were members of the Loreto Order, a seventeenth-century order of nuns which was dedicated to the education of women. The headquarters of this order were in Rathfarnam, near Dublin, Ireland.

Agnes contacted the Loreto Sisters in Ireland and asked to be accepted into their organization. She explained that her goal was to work with the Sisters in Bengal. She was given permission to join the organization, but she was told that she would first have to come to the Loreto Abbey in Rathfarnam, to learn English.

On 26 September 1928, young Agnes left her home in Skopje. her family. Though she did not know it, she would never see her mother again. She would return to Skopje only more than half a century later, in 1980, to set up a Home for poor, elderly and sick people. By this time, her mother was no longer alive.

COMING TO INDIA

Agnes spent about two months at the Loreto Abbey. She did not have much chance of interacting with the Loreto Sisters. This was partly because her command of English was very minimal, and because her time was fully taken up by learning the language.

Agnes had been accompanied to Rathfarnam by another Yugoslavian girl, who was also headed to India. But this girl was also a stranger. During these months, Agnes was alone for the first time in her life, without her beloved family, in a new place where the culture and language were very different from what she was accustomed to. She was excited and a little bewildered at the same time. But she remained focused on her task. She had come here with a purpose, and this was only the beginning of a long journey.

In November 1928, Agnes and her companion left by sea for India. They spent seven weeks on the ship. Though Agnes was very excited to be finally fulfilling her dream, she was also lonely and uncertain. She missed her home and her old life, and she did not know whether she would ever see her family again. Everything familiar was being left behind as she headed for a new land, with little idea of what awaited her. She turned to God again and again to seek strength on the journey.

The ship docked at Bombay. From here, Agnes and her companion had to catch a train to Calcutta. On 6 January 1929, Agnes finally arrived at Howrah station in Calcutta.

The sights, sounds and smells that greeted Agnes at the station must have been beyond anything she could have imagined: the crowded platform, coolies running to and fro, piles of luggage, people boarding the trains, *chaiwallahs* selling hot tea and snacks, people shouting out to each other ... But at the same time, she was thrilled. She had finally arrived. It was amongst these people that she had come to work, and to start her new life.

After a few days in Calcutta, Agnes was sent to the Loreto Convent, located at the hill station of Darjeeling, about 400 miles north of Calcutta. For the next two years, she would be trained as a novice. After completion of this training, she would take her vows to formally become a nun and a member of the Order.

Darjeeling was a beautiful town. It was situated at a height of 7,000 feet and surrounded by snow-clad peaks. The mountain air was crisp and refreshing. While the capital of British India was in Calcutta (until 1911), this had been the summer retreat for British men and women posted in Calcutta. At that time, there were several well-known schools there set up by British missionaries. Loreto Convent was one of these.

For the next two years, Agnes studied the scriptures and was trained to become a teacher, as that was the work she would have to undertake once she became a member of the Loreto Order. As part of her training, Agnes and the other novices had to teach poor children for two hours each day. Agnes, who always enjoyed teaching, enjoyed herself thoroughly. She continued mastering English and also learnt Bengali. As she was going to work in Calcutta, and wanted to work with poor people there, she felt that being fluent in Bengali was essential.

At the end of her novitiate in Darjeeling, Agnes took her first vows, which marked the formal beginning of her life as a nun. These were vows of poverty, chastity and obedience. Henceforth, she would have few material possessions; she was 'married' to God, and she would devote her life to serving Him completely and selflessly.

As part of the new life into which a nun enters after taking her vows, she is given a new name. Agnes chose the name of a French saint, Thérèse of Lisieux.

Thérèse (1873–97) was a French nun, who joined the Carmelite Order at the age of sixteen. She greatly admired the work of missionaries who travelled to different parts of the world to work with the poor. But her health prevented her from joining in the work herself, and she died of tuberculosis at the age of twenty-four. She was declared the patron saint for foreign missions in 1927.

Thérèse was also known for what is called her 'little way'. As she lived within the confines of the Carmelite Convent, Thérèse realized that she would not be able to achieve the 'great deeds' saints do and thus needed to find another way to express her love of God. As she wrote, 'Love proves itself by deeds, so how am I to show my love? Great deeds are forbidden me. The only way I can prove my love is by scattering flowers and these flowers are every little sacrifice, every glance and word, and the doing of the least actions for love.'

Agnes had been deeply inspired by the story of this young nun. She wanted to take Thérèse as her new name. However, as there was already another nun in the Convent called Thérèse, Agnes adopted the Spanish form of this name, 'Teresa', to prevent confusion. This would be the name by which people all over the world would come to know her.

Mother Teresa always stated that she had taken this name

not from the famous St. Teresa of Avila, but the 'little one', Thérèse of Lisieux. This choice spoke of her sense of her own humility and simplicity.

'THE HAPPIEST NUN IN THE WORLD'

Sister Teresa returned to Calcutta in the summer of 1931. She was sent to teach at St. Mary's School, a part of the Loreto Convent, located at Entally. Loreto Convent is still in existence, and is a well-known school in Calcutta.

The Convent is located in a quiet backstreet in the crowded central part of the city. It is surrounded by high grey walls with tall iron gates. Inside there are several buildings, ranging in style from gracious, old colonial to modern classroom blocks. There are large playing fields, tall trees and neatly kept lawns.

St. Mary's School stood within the Convent grounds. On its rolls were several hundred children who were taught in Bengali, including approximately 300 boarders. The boarders were often orphans or children whose parents could not afford to look after them.

Sister Teresa was twenty-one when she started work at St. Mary's. She would spend the next seventeen years of her life here. As she said later, 'In Loreto, I was the happiest nun in the world.'[*] Initially, she taught geography and history. Later, she would become the principal of the school.

---

[*] Jose Luis Gonzalez-Balado and Janet N. Playfoot, ed., *My Life for the Poor: Mother Teresa of Calcutta* (Ballantine Books, 1985).

The workday was long. Classes were from 9 a.m. to 3 p.m. In the evening, she had to correct the day's classwork, and then supervise the boarders' recreational activities. Her colleagues from those days remember her as very hard-working and always punctual. She was also strict about personal hygiene. It was her responsibility to oversee the students' baths and she made sure that they bathed well. Through her life, good hygiene remained an important concern.

In 1937, Sister Teresa took her final vows in Darjeeling. From now on, she was to be called Mother Teresa.

In the mid-1940s, Mother Teresa became the principal of St. Mary's. Her duties and responsibilities increased. The day would start at 4 a.m. with meditation, followed by Mass and then school prayers. After this, she would supervise the morning activities of the children. She also continued to teach her classes, along with the office and administrative work that came with the new position. In the evening there were prayers again, as well as supervision of the boarders' activities and their evening meal.

Despite the hard work and long hours, Mother Teresa enjoyed her work immensely. She was where she had wanted to be, doing the work she loved, living her life for God.

During these seventeen years, Mother Teresa's life and work were restricted to the school. She and the other nuns rarely ever went out of the Loreto Convent, because the rules of the Order were that nuns were to live a cloistered life, within the walls of the Convent. The thought of working on the streets of Calcutta did not occur to her. She had come to India to work with the poor, and that is what she was doing within the setting of the Convent.

A NEW DIRECTION

On 10 September 1946, Mother Teresa was on her way to Darjeeling by train. She was going on a retreat. Once a year, the Loreto nuns would go for a retreat, a period of silence and prayer. The purpose of the retreat was to communicate with God, to receive His guidance and to renew the vows that each nun had taken. Renewing vows gave strength and made the chosen path clear to the nuns once again.

While on the train, an event occurred that was to transform her life. She explained many years later: 'It was on that train that I heard the Call to give up all and follow Him into the slums—to serve Him in the poorest of the poor. I knew it was His will and that I had to follow Him . . . The message was quite clear. I was to leave the Convent and work with the poor while living among them. It was an order.'[*]

Mother Teresa understood that God now wanted something more from her. It was no longer enough for her to devote her life to Him while living in the Convent. He now wanted her to live and work with the poorest of the poor people, wherever they lived—on the streets, in the slums in the poorest and dirtiest

---

* Eileen Egan, *Such a Vision of the Street: Mother Teresa—The Spirit and the Work* (Sidgwick & Jackson, 1986).

parts of the city. He wanted her to go to all those places where no one else went, to comfort the poor people whom no one else cared for or wanted. She said, 'I felt that God wanted from me something more. He wanted me to be poor with the poor and love Him in the distressing disguise of the poorest of the poor.'[*]

In order to live and work with the poor, Mother Teresa would have to be poor herself. There could be no difference between her and those she was to serve. She had to experience poverty herself to be able to truly understand poor people and their needs.

During these years at the Convent, Mother Teresa had been saddened by the condition of the poor people on the streets. While the nuns lived a simple life, there was still enough for them to live on. As Mother Teresa said years later, 'I felt it very deeply that I should be snug in my bed and that on the road there should be those who have no shelter. I think it is wrong not to share.'

Mother Teresa now knew what she had to do, but she had no idea how to set about doing it. For a start, she had to get permission from her Order and from the Church, as the Sisters are meant to live and work within the Convent to which they belong. It was not possible for nuns to work outside on the streets while they belonged to any Order. She did not know if she would get this permission. She was also uncertain as to how she was going to start working on the streets and helping the poor.

The one thing Mother Teresa knew with great certainty was that somehow He would make it possible for her to do His work. Armed with her faith, she had to do her best, and He would be able to make this dream a reality.

On her return from Darjeeling, Mother Teresa went to see her

---

[*] Gonzalez-Balado and Playfoot, ed., *My Life for the Poor: Mother Teresa of Calcutta.*

spiritual adviser, Father van Exem. A Belgian priest who had come to Calcutta during World War II, Father van Exem had first met Mother Teresa in July 1944 in Calcutta. Soon after, he had been appointed her spiritual adviser, whom she consulted if she was facing any problem or dilemma.

When Mother Teresa revealed to Father van Exem what had happened on the train to Darjeeling, he was excited and very supportive. He was convinced that this was indeed a true message from God. But as he explained to her, she would need to get permission from various authorities before she could leave the Convent for a world outside it. Permission would be needed from the Loreto Order, the Church in India and the Vatican itself. They both realized that it was not going to be an easy process.

However, Father van Exem plunged into the work with enthusiasm. He first spoke to the Archbishop of Calcutta. Archbishop Perier was not at all happy with the request. No nun had ever left the safety and seclusion of the Convent to live and work in the outside world before. Although they did make visits outside, these were only brief outings to the doctor perhaps, or on their way to a retreat. Moreover, the Archbishop felt that it was not safe for a single woman, especially a European, to work in the city on her own.

The Archbishop told Father van Exem that he would think about the matter. He was a careful man and did not do things in haste. But he also told Mother Teresa that she should keep her plan a secret and not talk about it to anyone. Over the next few months, the Archbishop consulted various members of the Church. Some of them felt that it was possible for Mother Teresa to go ahead with her plan. It was only towards the end of 1947 that he gave Mother Teresa permission to write to the head of the Loreto Order about her plan.

Mother Teresa wrote to the Mother General at Loreto Abbey.

'Mother Teresa going to India' *by Katyayani Sinha, aged eight*

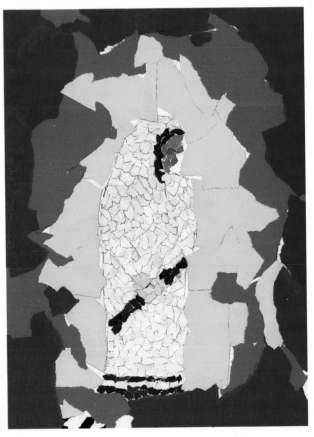

'Mother Teresa' *by Suryanandini Sinha*

She explained what had happened and that she was sure it was God's will that she go out and work with poor people. For this she would have to leave the Loreto Order permanently. But she wanted to remain a nun.

The Mother General understood. Within a few weeks—the letters went by sea and so took time to reach—she wrote back to Mother Teresa and gave her permission to write to the Vatican about her plan. She wholeheartedly supported Mother Teresa's intention to remain a nun.

There was one final and most important permission to be secured—and this was from the Vatican in Rome, where the authority of the Roman Catholic Church rested. If they refused permission, then no one could gainsay that.

Several more months went by, while Mother Teresa and Father van Exem waited eagerly for some news from Rome. Despite the long delay, Mother Teresa refused to give up hope. She prayed constantly and fervently.

At the end of July 1948, the Archbishop summoned Father van Exem and broke the news to him. Mother Teresa had been given permission by the Vatican to leave the Convent. She could work outside and continue to remain a nun. Her prayers had been answered!

However, there was one condition. Mother Teresa would be given permission to do her work outside for one year. This period would serve as a trial for her. At the end of that year, it was up to the Archbishop to decide if she could continue her work or return to the Convent. She had to prove that she was capable of the difficult task she had set out to do. The questions were many: Would she have the strength and courage to take care of not just herself, but also the poor people? How would she support herself? Would she remain safe and healthy? The Archbishop did not know the answers to all these questions. Only time would reveal them.

It was only on 8 August 1948 that the Archbishop gave Father van Exem permission to break the news to Mother Teresa. When she heard the news, she rushed to the chapel to pray. Then she asked Father van Exem if she could begin her work. She wanted to start work immediately!

That evening, Mother Teresa went to Father van Exem. He gave her three identical white saris with blue borders. These saris were similar to those worn by women in Calcutta who cleaned the streets and did other menial tasks. This was going to be Mother Teresa's new habit. She wore such a sari for the rest of her life, and it also became the uniform for all her Sisters to this day. As a result, no matter where one is, one can immediately recognize a Missionaries of Charity Sister by her sari.

Father van Exem blessed Mother Teresa's new habit and gave her a rosary. She asked him to write to her mother in Skopje to inform her that although she was leaving the Loreto Convent to step out into the world of the poor, she was doing so with her religious vows intact.

Father van Exem suggested to Mother Teresa that before she began to work with the poor, she needed to get basic medical training, to learn how to deal with malnutrition and the diseases that she would encounter on the streets. With such training, she would be better equipped to treat the poor people. When she agreed, he wrote to the Medical Mission Sisters in Patna, in the neighbouring state of Bihar, who ran their own hospital. They were willing to give Mother Teresa the necessary medical training.

Meanwhile, the Archbishop had letters sent out to every Loreto institution in India, giving the news about Mother Teresa, and asking everyone to pray for her.

On 17 August 1948, as she left for Patna, Mother Teresa wore her white sari for the first time. For the last seventeen years, she had worn the habit of the Loreto Order: a long black tunic, with a wimple, coif and veil. Father van Exem pinned a cross on her sari, which she wore every day henceforth. Mother Teresa had never worn a sari before, but it is what she chose to wear for the rest of her life. Her life was going to be spent among the poor, and she wanted to wear clothes that they were familiar with. She wanted to be as close as possible to them in every way, and this was one of them.

Mother Teresa spent a few months at the hospital in Patna. She learnt how to treat accidents and emergency cases, to assist in surgery and deliver babies. She worked with the nurses to learn how to take care of the patients in the wards, give injections and to prescribe medicines for minor illnesses. She saw people suffer a lot, but she did not flinch from the sight of blood. She also saw patients die, but she was not scared or discouraged by this experience. She worked very hard at the hospital and thoroughly enjoyed her medical training.

During the evenings, when there was some free time, the nuns at the hospital would discuss Mother Teresa's plans with her. They gave her good practical advice, based on their experience of caring for the sick. For example, Mother Teresa wanted to eat the food that poor people ate—boiled rice with salt—as another way of affirming that she was sharing their life and suffering. She did not want to eat better food than they did. However, the Patna nuns disagreed with her. They said that on that diet, she too would fall ill and be unable to take care of the poor. She could eat simple, inexpensive food, but she had to make sure there was enough nutritional value in what she ate.

The Patna nuns also told her that in her long day of work, it was very important that she take some time to rest every afternoon. Personal hygiene was very important to prevent illness. They advised Mother Teresa to cover her head with her sari because the heat in summer was unbearable and the head needed to be covered for protection.

Mother Teresa never forgot the advice the Patna Sisters gave her and followed it faithfully. Once she set up her Order, all the Sisters too had to follow these directives. To this day, the Sisters eat simple but nourishing meals, rest every afternoon for a little while and keep their heads covered. They each have three identical saris: one to wear, one to wash, and the third one to keep for emergencies or special occasions.

After a few weeks of being at the hospital, Mother Teresa was already impatient to go back to Calcutta and start her work. In November, Father van Exem came to visit her in Patna.

Mother Teresa told Father van Exem that she was ready to go back to Calcutta. He believed that she needed more training. But when he asked the senior Sisters at the hospital, they agreed that Mother Teresa was indeed ready and she could go back to Calcutta.

A HUMBLE BEGINNING

Mother Teresa returned to Calcutta on 9 December 1948. But she did not return to the Loreto Convent. It was not easy for her to return to the familiar city but not to her beloved Convent. She had spent over seventeen years there, and it was the only home she had known in India. Later, she said that leaving Loreto was even tougher than leaving her home and family in Skopje. The Loreto Sisters would continue to help Mother Teresa in various ways in the early years after she left the Order. They also offered her financial help. However, she refused to take money from them except for a mere five-rupee note.

Father van Exem had arranged for Mother Teresa to live with the Little Sisters of the Poor, a religious group that also believed in living a life of poverty. These Sisters ran the St. Joseph's Home for the aged, where they looked after about 200 poor elderly people. As their work was similar to what Mother Teresa wanted to do, this was felt to be a good introduction to her new life.

For a few days, Mother Teresa helped the Sisters with their work at St. Joseph's. Then, on 20 December, she decided it was time to start her own work.

She chose to begin in a slum called Motijhil, an hour's walk from St. Joseph's Home. In the middle of this slum was a large tank full of water that the people of the area used for drinking and washing. Surrounding the tank were lots of huts. The whole place was filthy, with garbage lying all around. Sewage flowed through open drains that ran past the huts.

All this did not affect Mother Teresa. What she saw was poverty, disease and helplessness, and her heart went out to the people there.

Mother Teresa started her work at Motijhil by doing what she did best: teach. She wanted to start by running a small school for the children of the slum. The people there did not have money to send their children to school. Nor was there any free school nearby.

Mother Teresa wondered how to get students, but this problem was solved by Father Henry, a friend of Father van Exem's, who was very supportive of Mother Teresa's mission. Father Henry knew several poor families in Motijhil, and he put her in touch with them. She found these families in the slum and told them that she wanted to teach their children. These parents were happy at the thought of a little school and promised to send their children to her the very next day.

The following morning, Mother Teresa arrived at the slum to find five children waiting for her. But there was a small problem. She had no blackboard, no chalk, no books, no furniture and no classroom! Nor did she have the money to buy any of these things.

But she remained unperturbed. She believed firmly that God would take care of her and the work He wanted her to do. Without a second thought, she picked up a stick lying nearby and began to scratch the letters of the Bengali alphabet on the ground. This was the start of her little school in Motijhil.

That day—21 December 1948—was the true beginning of Mother Teresa's new life. Though the Missionaries of Charity was formally founded on 7 October 1950 when the Vatican approved its constitution, this day was the start of an endeavour that would change the lives of millions.

The problem of scarce resources, which would have daunted others, never overly worried her. She was always sure that the means would arrive. And this belief was repeatedly proved true. A few days after Mother Teresa started work at Motijhil, she went to visit a priest in the locality of Park Circus. He gave her a hundred rupees to help her work.

Mother Teresa was delighted. She promptly rented two rooms in the slum, right in front of the tank. She made one room into a classroom for the children and converted the other into a dispensary where she could treat the sick people in the slum. The rent for the rooms was five rupees each. She could not start using them immediately because they needed repairs and cleaning. So she continued to hold classes outside. Fortunately, it was winter so it was quite comfortable in the open.

By the end of December, there were twenty-one children in the school. As the news of her little school spread to the Loreto community, her lay teacher friends and students came to see her. Some of them even burst into tears when they saw their former principal dressed in a simple sari, teaching the slum children without any assistance. Over a period of time, several of them volunteered their services to Mother Teresa whenever they were free.

Meanwhile, Mother Teresa was thoroughly enjoying herself with the children. As always, she continued to be concerned about cleanliness. She began to teach the children about basic hygiene. As at St. Mary's, she supervised their baths every day. The children who were the cleanest, and those who attended school most regularly were rewarded with prizes of bars of soap.

Mother Teresa started to try systematically to acquire

medicines, food and old clothes—all the materials she required for her work. She often walked long distances to try to find people willing to donate what she needed. As she walked, she often reflected on how hard life must be for the poor and destitute who had to spend every day hoping desperately that someone would offer them some food or money in order to survive.

Though she had some money set aside for her daily tram ride, Mother Teresa usually spent this money to buy medicines or food for some poor person who needed it urgently. The walk to Motijhil from St. Joseph's was a long one. As a result, Mother Teresa would be completely worn out by the end of the day. Therefore, she started to look for a place to live near Motijhil. But though she liked a few places, somehow they never seemed to work out.

The people of Motijhil began to appreciate Mother Teresa's efforts to help them. As the days passed, and they saw that Mother Teresa was striving hard for the welfare of their children, they began to help her in small ways. Someone brought some chalks and a slate. Somebody else donated a little bit of money or a small table. Other people brought along some books. Every morning, the children would rush to meet her as she entered the slum, long before the classes started.

By 4 January 1949, Mother Teresa had three more teachers to help her. There were now fifty-six children in the school. By 14 January, the schoolroom was ready and the classes shifted indoors.

The children were given Bengali and mathematics lessons. The girls were taught sewing as well, which they really enjoyed as they could now help their mothers at home. The children were naturally bright, and with Mother Teresa's love and encouragement, they showed much improvement in their studies.

That was not the only improvement. The children were accustomed to hearing the adults around them use crude language. However, they spontaneously decided to stop using such language. One day, the children brought one of their classmates to Mother Teresa because he had been rude and used foul language when speaking to his mother. Mother Teresa told him that the school did not like children who abused their mothers. The boy was very remorseful.

Mother Teresa's work began to grow as her reputation spread. People began to hear of a sari-clad nun who was helping the poor and started coming to her for help from nearby areas. The poor people of Tiljala, a neighbouring slum, also wanted her to set up a school and a dispensary for them.

There were many sick people to be tended to and Mother Teresa needed to procure medicines. As she was a very practical person, she decided that the best way to get them would be to start begging for medicines. She visited chemists and other shopkeepers and asked them for whatever medicines or general supplies they could spare. Sometimes they helped her, but at other times they would turn her away. She did not take these rejections badly or feel humiliated. She accepted them as God's will. But as the days went by, more and more people began to help her in whatever way they could. This enabled her work to grow. She was now busy from morning till night. It was exhausting, but it also gave her immense happiness.

In these early days, Mother Teresa kept a journal where she wrote her experiences. Often these entries were quite short, but very revealing. On 16 February 1949, for example, she wrote, 'But today I learnt a good lesson—the poverty of the poor must be often so hard for them. When I went around looking for a home, I walked and walked till my legs and arms ached. I thought how they must also ache in body and soul looking for home, food, help.'*

Occasionally, she experienced a longing for the comfort and companionship of the life she had left behind at the Convent. But she fought the temptation to take the easy path. 'Of free choice, my God, and out of love for You, I desire to remain and do whatever be Your Holy Will in my regard. I did not let a single tear come, even if I suffer more than now ... My God, give me courage now, this moment, to persevere in following Your will.'

---

*   Navin Chawla, *Mother Teresa* (Penguin Books India, 1993).

THE EARLY DAYS

As Mother Teresa continued her work in the slums, Father van Exem realized that Mother Teresa needed a place to stay that was closer to Motijhil, so she would not have to spend two hours a day walking to and fro from St. Joseph's. He and Father Henry cycled all over, looking for a suitable place. But as Mother Teresa had found before, there seemed nothing that was suitable.

Then Father van Exem had an idea. He knew two brothers called Alfred and Michael Gomes who lived in a large three-storeyed house at 14 Creek Lane. The top floor was unoccupied. He asked Alfred if Mother Teresa could move in. Alfred had already heard of Mother Teresa and the work she was doing. He discussed the matter with Michael and their other brothers, and they agreed to give a large room on the top floor to Mother Teresa.

On 28 February 1949, Mother Teresa moved into her new home with her meagre belongings. But the move, while very practical, brought its own problems. She discovered that she was very lonely. Life at the Convent had meant that she had companions who could comfort and support her. The organization lent a stable framework to their lives. The Convent provided protection to all who lived within it. Even at St. Joseph's, the other nuns around her had been doing similar work, and she could discuss her work and problems with them. They had prayed together and taken their evening meals together.

From this life of support, companionship and certainty, Mother Teresa suddenly found herself all alone and adrift. Her future seemed uncertain. She had no concrete plan regarding her work with the poor. She said, 'I was on the street, with no shelter, no company, no helper, no money, no employment, no promise, no guarantee, no security.'[*]

This was also the first time she was experiencing real poverty. Though she had had very few possessions at Loreto, the basic necessities of life—shelter, food, clothing and other essentials—had been provided for by the Convent. Though Mother Teresa never doubted that her decision to leave Loreto and live on the streets was right, it was a very hard and lonely path she had chosen for herself.

The Gomes brothers tried to make Mother Teresa comfortable. They offered her their spare furniture to furnish the bare room, but she accepted only a chair and some boxes that she used as tables as well as seats.

Mother Teresa's daily journey to Motijhil was much less arduous now. She could devote more time and energy to her 'begging expeditions'. These involved long walks where she went to places to seek food, clothes and medicines for her charges. Occasionally, Michael Gomes would accompany her on these rounds. As he recalls, she would come to him and say, 'Michael, can you come out with me? I want to go on a begging expedition.' His eight-year-old daughter Mabel became Mother Teresa's companion on begging expeditions as well as on visits to Motijhil.

Mabel loved Mother Teresa dearly and thought that the work

---

[*]   Gonzalez-Balado and Playfoot, ed., *My Life for the Poor: Mother Teresa of Calcutta.*

she was doing was very special. Mother Teresa was glad to have Mabel with her, not just for her company but because Mabel instinctively loved the poor. Mother Teresa would watch approvingly as Mabel helped her care for the poor and sick.

When it came to feeding the poor, sometimes Mother Teresa would give them her own food because she could not find food for them. She would go hungry instead. Poor and sick people also began to come to the gates of 14 Creek Lane, looking for Mother Teresa.

On 1 March, Mother Teresa heard a knock on her door. She found a former student from St. Mary's waiting outside. Subashini Das was one of the older students whom Mother Teresa had motivated to visit slums to teach the children and to visit poor patients in the hospitals. After moving into Creek Lane, Mother Teresa had written to Subashini, asking her to come and meet her.

Subashini said that she had come to join Mother Teresa in her new life. Mother Teresa warned her that it was a hard life and asked her if she was prepared for it. Subashini said, 'I know it will be hard; I am prepared for it.'* Mother Teresa asked her to think about it and then, if she wanted, to come back on 19 March.

On that day, at the appointed time, Subashini arrived at Mother Teresa's door. She was the first Sister to join Mother Teresa's organization, and she spent the rest of her life working side by side with Mother Teresa in the service of the poor. In a touching gesture, Subashini took the name Agnes, Mother Teresa's earlier name, when she became a nun. She was to remain Mother Teresa's lifelong companion. Mother Teresa was by her side when she died on 9 April 1997.

---

* Gonzalez-Balado and Playfoot, ed., *My Life for the Poor: Mother Teresa of Calcutta*.

Subashini's arrival at Creek Lane was an important moment for Mother Teresa. Though she was not afraid to work alone, she knew that the work required many more people. She saw Subashini's appearance as a blessing from God, an indication that she was on the right path.

A few weeks later, another former student from St. Mary's School came to join Mother Teresa. Magdalena Gomes took the name Sister Gertrude.

Mother Teresa was delighted with her two new Sisters. She encouraged both girls to study. Sister Agnes was in the middle of a teacher-training course, which Mother Teresa wanted her to finish. Mother Teresa persuaded Sister Gertrude to study medicine. Her few months of training with the Sisters in Patna had made her realize the importance of having a qualified doctor for their work. Sister Gertrude would eventually come third in West Bengal in her final MBBS examination.

The three Sisters continued their work in the slums. There was still very little money. Sometimes there was no food, but that did not trouble them too much. When they were hungry, Mother Teresa would occasionally ask Michael Gomes for a cup of rice which he would readily give.

Over the next few months, several more Sisters joined Mother Teresa. The Gomes brothers got used to hearing the sounds of their laughter in the evenings when they all came back home. It was like one big family upstairs and Mother Teresa and her Sisters were happy with their new life.

When Mother Teresa started her work with the poor people, she added another vow to the ones she had taken when she became a nun. Later, every Sister who joined the Missionaries of Charity also took this vow. This was the vow of 'wholehearted and free service to the poorest of the poor'. This vow was fundamental to the work that Mother Teresa and her Sisters would do. Working with the poor required courage, endurance and a cheerful nature. The Sisters had to be completely dedicated to their work, otherwise it would not be possible to continue it day after day. It was also important that the services to the poor be free. Mother Teresa and her Sisters never took any payment from the poor. This was a condition that Mother Teresa was very firm about.

THE MISSIONARIES OF CHARITY

When Mother Teresa laid the seed of her organization in Motijhil, she had little idea that it would one day grow to spread across the world. She always said that she was merely a pencil in the hands of the Lord. He wrote, through her. It gave her great joy that God chose to do His work through her.

As Mother Teresa's group grew larger, they all waited for the day that they could become a formal organization, recognized by the Church in India as well as the Vatican.

By early 1950, a few months after Mother Teresa started her work in Motijhil, Archbishop Perier decided to accept Mother Teresa's desire for such an organization. He asked Father van Exem to write the constitution for the organization and submit it to him as soon as possible. He was travelling to Rome in April and he wanted to present the Church officials with the constitution. They would have to give the final approval.

Father van Exem developed the constitution. Every organization approved by the Catholic Church has to have a formal constitution listing the rules and beliefs that guide it. He based these rules on existing Church laws as well as on Mother Teresa's own beliefs and experience. The rules therefore included the fact that members of the organization had to live like the poor and work among them. They could only set up institutions

'Mother Teresa helping poor children on the streets' *by Katyayani Sinha*

'Mother Teresa brings colour to children's lives' *by **Katyayani Sinha***

or Homes for vulnerable people who could not take care of themselves, such as children, the elderly, the very sick and dying, and the mentally ill. The vow of 'wholehearted and free service' to the poorest of the poor was also included.

On 7 October 1950, the Vatican formally approved the constitution. The Missionaries of Charity came into official existence.

With the establishment of the Missionaries of Charity, the work was formalized and new rules were laid down. No Sister was allowed to go out alone; she had to be accompanied by another Sister. Even when Mother Teresa went out into the streets, she was accompanied by at least one other Sister, depending on where she was going and the nature of the work there. If there was a particular poor colony or slum where there were many poor people who needed food, medical treatment and other kinds of help, more Sisters would go along.

Mother Teresa remembered clearly how lonely and vulnerable she sometimes felt in the early days, when she had wished she had a companion by her side. It was also much safer. A single woman walking by herself in poor areas could become a target to someone's anger, rudeness or hostility. From the Creek Lane days, she had started going out with a companion whenever possible, usually Michael Gomes or his daughter Mabel.

Young women came from all over the country to join the Missionaries of Charity. As more people joined the organization, the Gomeses let Mother Teresa occupy all the rooms on the top floor. However, over the next two years, even this proved too small and Mother Teresa realized that she would have to look for a bigger place.

She found a large house at 54A Lower Circular Road. Mother Teresa and her Sisters, now twenty-seven in number, moved there in February 1953. This house was named Motherhouse.

A narrow side street led up to the door. Outside, there was a bell that one had to pull, and it would set off a delicate ringing sound. As soon as it was rung, the door would be opened by a Sister. There was a sign outside the door, which had Mother Teresa's name on it. Below it was a shutter that could be moved to the 'in' or 'out' position, which was used to indicate where Mother was.

Upon entry, there was a parlour on the left, where visitors were shown in. It was simply furnished with a table, some benches and cotton curtains at the windows. Beyond the parlour was a large courtyard with a well at one end. Water from this well was used for bathing, drinking and cooking as well as washing utensils and clothes.

Upstairs, there was a large hall. This was the chapel. It had a simple altar with statues of Jesus Christ and the Virgin Mary. The chapel was bright and airy, with lots of windows that overlooked Lower Circular Road. Though this was a busy road, and traffic has only increased over the years, somehow the noise coming through the windows never disturbed the peace and serenity of the chapel.

I began to visit Motherhouse in the 1990s, and always felt a sense of tranquillity when I sat on the cool earthen floor of this chapel. I would attend evening prayers there occasionally. Morning Mass was held very early in the morning and I never managed to wake up on time to attend it. Once, Mother Teresa, with a twinkle in her eye, asked me to come for morning Mass. My heart sank at the thought of waking up so early. She started laughing, as though guessing my thoughts, and said, '*Acha*, come in the evening then!'

Mother Teresa would sit at the back of the room in her customary position on the floor, with her Sisters gathered around her as they prayed. The Sisters would also sing hymns. I did not know the words so I could not join in, but hearing the sweet voices filled me with joy. Visitors were always welcome during the prayers—local people, as well as visitors from other parts of the country and even abroad, would come and attend them.

Mother Teresa and the Sisters had their living quarters on the first floor. The office, once the work of the Missionaries of Charity became widespread, was also located on this floor. Outside the office, there was a narrow corridor, with a couple of benches on either side. I recall sitting with Mother Teresa and my father on these benches while we chatted. Although the parlour was downstairs, visitors would still make their way up here to catch a glimpse of Mother Teresa or to simply touch her feet and receive her blessings.

One always thought of Mother Teresa as an Indian. Technically, she was—for she had taken Indian citizenship in 1950, when the Constitution came into existence. She spoke fluent Bengali and Hindi. With her simple white sari draped around her, her head covered like any traditional Indian woman's, one forgot that she had been born in a faraway country. Many people called her 'ma', and greeted her with a 'namaste' and touched her feet. She would say, '*Ami Bharater, Bharat amar.*' ('I belong to India and India belongs to me.')

There was a strong element of family feeling among the Sisters, who had left their families behind to join this Order that they believed in. They all looked upon Mother Teresa as their mother.

And so, a simple young Albanian girl was transformed into an Indian nun, a mother for the poor.

'A CHILD IS A GIFT OF GOD'

Mother Teresa loved children. To her, every child was special and had the right to be loved. She used to say, 'God's own image is in every child, no matter what that child is, disabled or beautiful or ugly—it's God's beautiful image created for greater things— to love and be loved . . . That little one who is unwanted and unloved, who has come into the world already unwanted, what a terrible suffering that is! Today, this is the greatest disease: to be unwanted, unloved, just left alone . . .'

Babies and little children were often abandoned on the streets, or left to die in gutters and dustbins. Sometimes, children were thrown out of their houses. At other times, parents left a child outside one of Mother Teresa's Homes, knowing that Mother Teresa and her Sisters would look after the child. If the police or a kind stranger found a child roaming the streets, abandoned and frightened, they would bring him or her to the Missionaries of Charity.

Children were abandoned for different reasons. In some cases, the parents were too poor to be able to look after their children and would simply abandon them. Parents occasionally rejected children because they had some physical or mental disability. Or the parents themselves could have died from starvation and illness, leaving their children helpless. Young girls were abandoned because their parents wanted sons.

As Mother Teresa worked in the streets of Calcutta, she discovered more and more such children. Finally, she decided that she would set up a Home where she and her Sisters could give such children proper care. In 1955, Mother Teresa set up her first children's Home in Calcutta, called the Nirmala Shishu Bhawan (Shishu Bhawan means 'home for children' in Hindi and Bengali). This Home was just down the road from Motherhouse.

After that, Shishu Bhawans were set up in many parts of India. The number of children in different Homes depended on the size of the building. The bigger Homes could accommodate about 200 children, the smallest ones about twenty.

Some years ago, I visited the Nirmala Shishu Bhawan one afternoon. This was my first trip to Calcutta after Mother Teresa's death.

The Home was very quiet; there were no children's voices. A passing Sister told me that it was children's naptime. In the parlour where I waited for Sister Marjorie, the walls were covered with children's drawings of Mother Teresa. Her photographs were also hung on the walls. Wherever I looked, I could see her!

A few minutes later, Sister Marjorie walked into the parlour. We talked for a while, and then she asked if I wanted to go and see the children. I nodded.

The nursery was on the first floor. It was a large airy room with cribs placed on one side of the room. There were toys scattered over the floor. The children were just waking up. Some of them were crying; others were ready to start playing. Seeing us, they rushed towards us. Sister Marjorie introduced me to various children and I spent some time playing with them. They were a joy to be with: full of love and laughter.

I wondered how these children felt when visitors, such as

me, spent time with them on one occasion and then perhaps never came back. Did they wonder why such people never returned? Did the children feel bad? It was so easy to get attached to someone, but so difficult when a child discovered that that person was not going to return. When I asked Sister Marjorie about this, she said, 'What about us? We [Sisters] move from one Home to another all the time . . . These children cannot afford attachments the way other people do. They have to become strong if they have to survive.'

I felt guilty. These children already had such difficult lives, and this was one more hardship for them. I must have looked rather anxious for Sister Marjorie said, 'To be with these children is to be loved. Just receive the love. That is all.'

Apart from being the biggest children's Home in the organization, Shishu Bhawan in Calcutta is also the main adoption centre of the Missionaries of Charity. Over the years, thousands of babies and little children have been given for adoption.

Though there may be hundreds of children in the nurseries, when parents come to select a child for adoption, they are only shown two or three. Prospective parents are not allowed into the nursery. This is because Mother Teresa did not like the idea of parents choosing among lots of babies. She did not want prospective parents to judge the child on his or her appearance or any other such reason. She wanted parents to accept a child because they were willing to love the child as he or she was. All children were equal, and all of them deserved the love of a mother and a father.

The parents, however, are carefully checked by the Sisters to make sure they are good people who would be able give the child a happy and stable home. Mother Teresa took great pains with every adoption she arranged. It was a great moment when she handed over an orphaned child to new parents and a new life. It gave her immense joy to know that one more child had been given the opportunity to live the kind of life he or she had the right to: the love of parents, a home and family, and a secure future.

The children from Shishu Bhawan were not only taken into Indian families, but also into families from all over the world. Many of the children given for adoption to families outside India are physically or mentally challenged. This is because health facilities are generally better in the western countries and there are better provisions for children with special needs. A lot of children from Shishu Bhawan have found new homes in Belgium, Italy and Switzerland. Sometimes, one set of parents adopt several children with special needs.

Prince was a little boy who Mother Teresa was very fond of. When Prince was a year and a half old, he was adopted by a Swiss couple, Mr and Mrs Ballestraz, who came from Sierre, Switzerland. Mr Ballestraz made tools and instruments for people with special needs. Little Prince had no hips and no legs. His hands, instead of falling normally, turned backwards. When the Ballestrazes saw this little boy, they decided that they had to take care of him and help him live as normal a life as possible. They made him a rubber 'hip' to which a pair of prosthetic legs were attached. Prince soon learnt to walk on his own. The Ballestraz family includes other children adopted from the Missionaries of Charity, namely Sabita, Maya, Sarjan, Sapna and Prem Kumari. All of them had severe physical or mental problems. Today, they are all part of the large and happy Ballestraz family.

Children are also sent for adoption from other Missionaries of Charity children's Homes. Among these is Shishu Bhawan in Commissioner's Lane, in north Delhi. At the end of a long, narrow lane, with old houses on either side, is a large gate that opens to a circular driveway lined with trees and flowering plants. This Shishu Bhawan is also a large house, with quite a number of babies and children living there. This was where Mother Teresa stayed whenever she was in the city.

I remember my first visit to Shishu Bhawan many years ago. It was during one of Mother Teresa's stays. I was standing near her, watching her as she spoke and laughed with people who had come to receive her blessings. Though her features were ordinary and her face deeply lined (she was in her 70s at this time), her face shone. She seemed to simply radiate light. I felt an immense peace wash over me. It was like standing in Divine presence.

Mother Teresa and the Sisters' quarters were in a separate section. I once saw Mother Teresa's room. It was tiny, with barely enough room to squeeze in a narrow bed, a desk and a chair. Mother Teresa did not spend much of her time sleeping. Over the years, as her work got busier and busier, she spared even less time to sleep. Late into the night, she would sit at her desk and painstakingly reply to the innumerable letters and notes that people sent her.

The children's Home that I was most familiar with was Jeevan Jyoti. I started visiting Jeevan Jyoti regularly in 1995. The children there became my companions.

Jeevan Jyoti was a big house. On the ground floor, near the parlour, was the chapel with the Virgin Mary's statue on the altar, along with an image of Jesus Christ. Long windows along one side let in light. There were dhurries on the ground for people to sit, and some chairs at the back for people who were unable to sit on the ground. There was a small bookshelf with prayer books and the Holy Bible. I would sit there for a while almost every day when I visited. Sometimes a visitor would bring fresh flowers that would be placed near the Virgin Mary's statue. In the morning and the evening, there would be prayers that were attended by most of the children, along with the Sisters and the girls who looked after the children. Also on the ground floor were the dormitory where the Sisters slept, their dining room, office and the kitchen.

At that time, there were about forty children at Jeevan Jyoti, ranging in age from infants to children of about twelve. Many of them were physically or mentally challenged. They shared three large rooms. In the first, most of the children between three and ten played and ate during the day. At night, it was converted into a bedroom. There was a large bed tucked away into a corner, which was shared by as many children that could pile on comfortably. The rest slept on mattresses on the floor.

The room beside this was for very young children, most of whom were suffering from severe mental and physical handicaps. These children were unable to get up or do anything for themselves. Many could not even speak or move. Initially, when I went into this room to see the little children in their cribs, I was shocked. Not only were they physically traumatized, but they also seemed locked in a lonely, silent world of their own. Gradually, as I spent time with them, I learnt their names, and was thrilled when some of them were able to respond by smiling.

The third room was the nursery, where the babies lived. The corridor that ran past these three rooms got converted into a playground of sorts during the day, with children running up and down, chasing each other and playing games. The children who could not move independently would be seated on the floor, or in stools or chairs, so that they too could enjoy the atmosphere.

We had wonderful times, the children, the Sisters and I, although the Sisters were always very busy. Being with these children was an experience very different from anything I had ever imagined. I had thought that it was I who was coming to help and to give. I was wrong. I was constantly receiving. The children gave me their love and laughter, their trust and their friendship. They made no demands of me. As I left every day, I felt I had been given a precious gift.

Amit and Ashok, who were about four years old, were the best of friends and practically inseparable. No one could resist Amit's charm or his smile! I could not understand why his parents had given him away, as he was in very good physical and mental health.

Upon my asking one of the Sisters, I was told that he had been born with both male and female organs. I wondered about the nature of human beings: we are so quick to reject those people and things that are not 'normal' in our perception.

Ashok, like Amit, was a sweet child, and he too had been rejected for a similar reason.

One evening, at teatime, the children had been given their share of biscuits and were happily munching them. Ashok suddenly started crying. When Amit went up to him and asked what was wrong, Ashok sobbed and said he had finished his biscuits. Amit immediately handed Ashok his own share, saying, 'Don't cry, have my biscuits!' I was taken aback. Even when one has plenty, it is sometimes hard to give, but to be able to give when one has almost nothing is an exceptional quality. This is one of the qualities about the destitute that Mother Teresa said touched her the most. I would see this among other children at Jeevan Jyoti too. They learnt early on to share everything—clothes, toys, stationery. No child claimed ownership of any particular thing.

Over the next months, both Amit and Ashok underwent corrective surgery. Soon after, a family from Belgium decided to adopt Amit. He was delighted when he found out, and he was the envy of the other children. But little Ashok was desolate when he heard he was going to be separated from his friend. The Sisters tried to persuade the family to adopt Ashok as well, but they wanted only one child.

Rani was eight or nine when I started visiting Jeevan Jyoti. She was thin, and her legs were bent and twisted beneath her body. She could not stand or walk but could only drag herself from place to place. While the other children would gather around any visitor or volunteer, Rani would sit quietly by herself and just watch. She never spoke or called out when I passed by, unlike other children who would demand attention.

Rani's story was a traumatic one. She contracted polio when she was young, and her legs became weak and thin. Her father used to beat little Rani. One day he beat her so badly that he broke her legs. Since then, Rani was not able to stand up.

One day, while the other children were busy playing some game, I sat down beside her. After telling her my name, I asked her what her name was. For a while she did not say anything. Then, very shyly, she whispered, 'Rani.' That was the only conversation I managed with her that day. But after that, I made it a point to sit with her each time I went to Jeevan Jyoti, and to draw her into the other children's games and laughter. Though Rani could not join them, I could see that she liked being a part of their fun.

On one occasion, when I sat down on the floor beside her, I saw Rani smile for the first time. The effect was magical. It was as if someone had opened the windows in a dark room and allowed golden sunshine to pour in! Her thin, dark face lit up and she looked beautiful. After that, my goal was to make shy little Rani smile as much as possible. Though she never spoke much, a smiling Rani made all of us happy.

The Sisters at Jeevan Jyoti used to get medical help for the handicapped children whenever possible. It was not easy because doctors were unable to come regularly. A doctor and a physiotherapist would sometimes drop in to treat children. But no one quite knew how to treat Rani because her legs were so badly maimed. We decided to take her to a big government hospital in Delhi so that a doctor I knew could examine her.

So, one morning, I arrived at Jeevan Jyoti to fetch Rani and Sister Ann Vinita. Rani was ready and waiting, very excited at the thought of an outing, even if it was to a hospital! She was dressed in a pretty frock with her hair neatly combed, smiling from ear to ear. As the three of us made our way out of the gate, the other children waved from the windows above, yelling in unison, 'Bye, bye!' Rani waved back happily.

When we arrived at the hospital, Sister Ann Vinita and I had to take turns carrying Rani to the doctor's room. After examining her, he decided to conduct some tests to check if she still had any life left in her legs. If she did, then perhaps there was hope of her being able to stand one day. The test the doctor had to conduct was a painful one because it involved pricking the skin with lots of needles. Sister Ann Vinita and I watched anxiously as the doctor began to push the needles into Rani's arms and legs. Each time a needle went in, I winced. But after a while I realized that though Sister Ann Vinita and I were worrying about her, Rani herself sat quietly, without a single whimper. Is it that Rani didn't cry because she felt no sensation in her legs?

We were very sad to find out that the condition of Rani's legs had deteriorated too far for anyone to help her. The nerves had atrophied, and once a nerve is dead, it cannot be revived again. Later, a sledge with wheels was made for her so that she could sit on it and move from place to place with ease instead of dragging herself. Despite the fact that there was little we could do to help her, Rani's lovely smile remained unchanged.

My house was near the Nizamuddin railway station in Delhi. About eight years ago, our cook Ram Kumar came to me one evening saying that there was a poor girl standing at the gate asking for help. She had come from the railway station nearby.

I went out of the house. In the fading light, she stood forlornly. She seemed about twelve years old. I brought her inside and asked her what had happened to her.

Her name was Salma and she was from a very poor family that lived in a village. She was unable to tell me what state she belonged to, unsure whether it was Madhya Pradesh, Bihar or Orissa. Some years earlier, her father had sent her to work with a middle-class couple in a nearby city. She did not know the name of the city. She used to look after the couple's children.

One day, this couple told her that they were going on a trip, and that she would have to accompany them. They did not tell her their destination. They spent many hours in the train. At one point, the train stopped at a station. Salma went to the toilet. When she returned to the compartment where they were all sitting, she discovered, to her horror, that it was empty. She looked everywhere for her employers but they were not to be found.

Terrified at being left alone, with no money and no knowledge even of where she was, Salma got off the train at that station. And the house where she made her way in desperation, turned out to be mine.

I gave Salma some food while I wondered what to do. I knew I had to help her, but how?

Suddenly, I had the answer. I explained to her as best as I could where I wanted to take her. I asked her if it was all right with her. Dazed, she nodded. I felt very sad for her. Salma, hungry, tired and scared, did not have many options anyway. But the place I had decided to take her to was a place I knew she would be safe and well looked after. It was Jeevan Jyoti.

When we arrived at the Home, it was dark. I took Salma in and called out to the Sisters, who came running. I quickly explained the situation to them. Without further ado, they took Salma in. Food, a bath and clean clothes made her feel a little better. Very tired, she went to sleep early that night. And that was how Salma came to live with the Missionaries of Charity. Once again, Mother Teresa had come to the rescue!

Today, Salma is a beautiful young woman. She hopes to get married and settle down, to finally have a home of her own and a family. She is now living with the Sisters at a Home in Jammu.

Recently, after a gap of several years, I went back to Jeevan Jyoti. The familiar building looked just as it had earlier. As I walked through the corridor, past the parlour and the chapel, I met a Sister. I asked to meet the Superior, Sister Kochu Thérèse, from whom I wanted permission before I went upstairs to meet the children.

Sister Kochu Thérèse very kindly escorted me upstairs. There, I ran into Sister Rosebella, who had been at Jeevan Jyoti when I used to visit earlier. When she took me to see the children, I looked around eagerly for people I knew.

In the first room, I recognized some of the children. They had been very small when I last saw them and did not recognize me. Little Harsha, who had been about four when I last saw her, seemed to have grown up fast. She had contracted polio as a little child, and now wore calipers to help her walk. She was smart, alert and always smiling. When I was here last, the Sisters had tried hard to get her adopted, and it seemed there was still no success.

Sister Rosebella introduced me to various children, who were doing their homework. She told me that most of the children at the Home were now going to school. Earlier, the Sisters had devoted much effort trying to find schools for the children. But it was not easy. The older children, who were illiterate, could not be placed in a junior class because they were far older than the other children in that class. The Sisters had been unable to find a school that would accept the older children, above the age of five for instance, in a nursery class. Also, it was not easy to find suitable schools for the handicapped children. At that time, the children's education had been limited to whenever a teacher could come and conduct classes occasionally. These classes were irregular and there was not much discipline. These teachers were mainly volunteers with other commitments as well. But over the years, the Sisters had managed to find schools willing to take in these children.

Sister Kochu Thérèse took me to see the study room, a small room located at one end of the corridor. A rather unusual class was going on. Several of the children were deaf and dumb. The two teachers were teaching them Hindi and English, using actions and gestures to convey the meaning of the words. The children had already learnt the alphabet and simple words, and were now forming sentences, which I could see scribbled in the notebooks in front of them. This was amazing!

The Sisters had clearly spared no effort to make sure that as many children as possible received an education. The numbers at Jeevan Jyoti had also gone up considerably. From about forty children some years ago, there were now about eighty. Several of these children had been placed in boarding schools.

All this while, I had been trying to catch a glimpse of Rani. I asked several people where she was, and finally I was told that she was playing on the swings downstairs. I peered through the windows in the corridor. In the large courtyard where the children played in the evenings, I could see some children on the swings, and finally glimpsed Rani. I decided to wait until she came upstairs.

In the meanwhile, I made my way to the nursery. I recognized two children, who had been infants when I last saw them. I was especially delighted to see Anthony. When he was born, his head had been filled with fluid which had to be continuously drained through a little pipe the doctors had put in. Nobody had expected that he would live very long. He was now a serious little boy of about four or five, busy doing his school homework when I met him. He did not recognize me and I am sure he was surprised at my joy at seeing him.

Reena was studying next to him. She was about the same age as Anthony, and she too had been a sick little baby. She had some blood disorder from birth and her limbs were wasting away. She was losing the power of her arms and legs, and Sister Rosebella told me there was no cure for her problem.

Sister Rosebella was tying bandages around the leg of a little girl who had just undergone corrective surgery for her crooked limbs. Sister told me that though this little girl was unable to use her arms and legs, she had learnt to draw using her mouth!

After Sister Rosebella had finished tying her bandages, she propped her up in a crib. Pillows were placed on her lap, and then a drawing book was placed on top of the pillows. Sister Rosebella put a pen in her mouth, and the little girl began to draw furiously, moving her head from side to side.

I was also introduced to Ramesh, who had to use crutches to walk but was learning to play the tabla, and fourteen-year-old Pooja, who was doing her BA in music while studying at school. The two of them performed together for me: Pooja sang, while Ramesh accompanied her.

'Mother Teresa's river of love' *by Katyayani Sinha*

'Mother Teresa spreads love to patients' *by Katyayani Sinha*

When I left the nursery after the music recital, I set out to find Rani. Suddenly I spotted her. She was smiling. She had recognized me. I was so happy. While I talked to her, Rani simply smiled. She had never been one for words! Her vocabulary was limited to just a few words. She was not much changed—she just looked a few years older.

As I finally got up to go, she said, '*Gadi.*' I immediately understood the significance of that word. In the earlier years, the children had a ritual. Whenever I was leaving Jeevan Jyoti, they would rush to the windows of their room, which overlooked the car park, to wave goodbye. As I would get into my vehicle, there was a chorus of voices saying 'Bye-bye!'

I was touched that Rani still remembered those goodbyes! I nodded to her and said, '*Gadi.*'

Then, she said, '*Kala.*' I was most surprised. In those days, the car that brought me to Jeevan Jyoti had indeed been black. She had not forgotten. I wonder where she had learnt the word 'kala'.

Smiling, I shook my head and said, '*Safed.*' The car I had come in today was white.

Rani said promptly, 'White.' My jaw dropped. I had never heard her speak a word of English before!

On my way out, I stopped at the chapel. I sat down to pray for a little while, for I was full of joy at being back here.

When I opened my eyes, it was to find that the room had filled up with children and visitors. It was time for the evening prayers. I slipped out quietly.

SISTERS AND BROTHERS

The Sisters of the Missionaries of Charity form the backbone of the organization. As the organization grew, more and more young, enthusiastic women joined. This meant that Mother Teresa could expand her work to even more countries. Sometimes the Sisters would be sent to big cities and sometimes to remote villages where there was no electricity or roads. But wherever Mother Teresa decided there was work to be done, wherever the poor needed their help, there they would go willingly.

The life of the Sisters is not easy. Like Mother Teresa, they too have given up their homes and families and sacrificed everything else to serve the poor. Once every ten years, the Sisters are allowed to go back and visit their families for a brief while. Otherwise, the only other time they can return to their families is if someone is gravely ill.

The Sisters rise very early in the morning. The day begins with Mass and meditation, followed by breakfast. The work differs from Home to Home, depending on location and whom they are caring for. But the general pattern remains much the same. They work all morning, either within the Home or outside in areas where people need food, medical treatment or counselling. They return for lunch and half an hour of rest, as the Sisters in Patna had recommended. After the rest, it's back to work. There are prayers in the evening, followed by whatever work needs to be done within the Home, and dinner. Then they offer the last prayers of the day, after which it is bedtime.

Though the work is hard, the Sisters work with joy. Whatever their task is—attending to a crying child, changing someone's bandages or feeding a sick person—they do it with love and patience. However busy they are, they always have time for whoever needs them. I have never seen any of the Sisters ignore someone's need because they were busy or tired. I do not know how they do it, and I can only watch in silent wonder.

Every kind of work is challenging. Those who work with the mentally ill need to attend to every detail of their physical care. The Sisters try to give as much love and support as they can. Some inmates need to be attended to for every small task. Others can manage to do things on their own, like going to the toilet, eating, bathing and so on. Similarly, the Sisters who work with the physically handicapped, both children and adults, have to cope with the patient's inability to care for himself or herself. Those at the children's Homes need to attend to the children's physical well-being as well as emotional needs, and try to provide education or vocational training. Leprosy patients require intensive medical care. They also need a lot of moral support from the Sisters because they often suffer from a lack of confidence in themselves, as leprosy has often been viewed with disgust and even horror by society.

Most of the leprosy patients are, however, looked after by the Brothers. The Brothers are priests who became a part of the Missionaries of Charity in 1963. Mother Teresa realized that there were certain tasks that the Sisters found difficult to do. There were places—such as the remote interiors of the country and in forests—where it was better to send men rather than women. She also saw that it would be best to have men look after boys who were growing up. Boys who had grown up on the streets and were now approaching adolescence required a firm hand to rehabilitate. The Brothers would best be able to handle such situations.

There are presently about 4,600 Sisters of the Missionaries of Charity all over the world, including India. There are far fewer Brothers—less than 400. The Brothers live in separate Homes, along with older boys and young men who were once living at the children's Homes. These boys are encouraged to get vocational training—in carpentry, motor maintenance and similar occupations—so that they can get jobs and support themselves.

When the children at the various Homes grow older, the Sisters and Brothers of the Missionaries of Charity try to arrange for their futures so that they can take care of themselves and lead fulfilling lives. Young men and women are taught vocational skills, and often jobs are found for them. The quality of education received in the various Homes differs, and those who have received a better education are placed in suitable jobs. Many of the young people, especially the girls, express the desire to get married. The Missionaries of Charity tries to find a suitable match for them. If they like each other, the wedding is arranged by the Sisters.

Though the Sisters cannot afford much, they try to give each girl a suitable trousseau and other wedding gifts, which are prepared with a lot of love and happiness. These weddings are very joyous events. All the people from the Home where the boy or girl has grown up are present. I have attended a couple of such weddings at Jeevan Jyoti. When one of the girls who helped to take care of the children was getting married, various friends and volunteers were also invited. It was a simple ceremony, with all the Sisters at Jeevan Jyoti watching lovingly. Afterwards, the

Sisters had organized a tea party. When it was time for the bride and groom to leave, the bride clung to the Sisters with tears pouring down her cheeks. She had not one but several mothers to say goodbye to! They all hugged her and wished her well in her new life.

The young men and women who marry and move into their own homes often come back to meet the Sisters. There is always great excitement when this happens. Everyone wants to see how the girls are looking in their saris and jewellery. Over the years, the Sisters and Brothers have looked on proudly as the young men and women they brought up and sent out into the world, return with their spouses and children to meet them. Many of these young people are doing very well in their jobs and return to their Homes to take the Sisters' blessings.

One of the illnesses that Mother Teresa was very concerned about was leprosy. Leprosy has affected countless people in India, especially the poor. It is a disease where the nerves in the afflicted parts of the body become atrophied and numb, usually in the hands, legs and nose. As a result, if there are cuts or burns in these areas, the patient cannot feel them. Slowly, these parts get infected, and begin to decay and rot away. At the last stages, the affected parts of the body even need to be amputated to prevent the spread of infection. Poor people have neither the awareness nor the means to attend to their medical problems, until it is too late.

Though leprosy has affected innumerable people all over the world for many centuries, it is now found only in the poor countries of Asia and Africa. Now there are medicines that can cure the disease completely if detected in the early stages. With increasing awareness, people are more conscious of the symptoms and seek treatment early. Leprosy-affected people begging for money are a common sight at the traffic lights in Delhi. They often have bandages on their hands and feet because now there are hospitals that are helping these poor patients.

Leprosy, since the earliest times, has been seen as something shameful and dirty. Many believed that someone gets leprosy because God has cursed him or her, and no one should go near such a person. Leprosy could be infectious if precautions are not taken, and so this was another reason why such people were shunned by society. Also, since the physical appearance of the patients was so dramatic, and since there was little available by way of treatment, leprosy patients were often thrown out of their homes, and sometimes even their villages or towns. At times, entire families who were affected by leprosy were banished from their villages. They had no opportunity to earn money, so lack of food and shelter made their condition worse. It was because of the pitiful position of the leprosy patients as a community that Mother Teresa focused on people suffering from this disease.

Until recently, many doctors and nurses did not want to treat people with leprosy because they felt that if they came near these patients, they too would contract the disease. There was no one to give them medicines or heal their wounds, and they would just watch in horror as the disease spread through their bodies.

Mother Teresa realized that not only were the leprosy patients living in miserable poverty, but also that there was no one to treat them or take care of them. They survived through begging, and suffered constant rejection from other people. Added to their physical discomfort was mental anguish and loneliness. Apart from the physical healing and treatment they urgently required, they needed to feel like human beings with a sense of self-worth. She believed that: 'Our leprosy patients are very beautiful people. If they have leprosy, then that . . . is God's gift. It is His way of bringing them closer to Himself.' To Mother Teresa, it was crucial that she, her Sisters and Brothers reach out to these unhappy human beings. She wanted to replace the shame and pain in their hearts with happiness and self-confidence.

Apart from food and medical care, Mother Teresa wanted the patients to realize that leprosy was only an illness, like any other, and God loved them very much. She felt that He gave them these problems so that they could remember Him and reach out to Him. He wanted them to learn to be brave and to have faith in Him.

In 1957, five people with leprosy arrived at Motherhouse. When their disease had been diagnosed, they had been thrown out of their jobs and turned away by their families. In desperation, they had come to Mother Teresa for help. She tried to rent a house in the city for them so that they could stay there, but the neighbours would not agree to this. This was when Mother Teresa first thought of a proper Home for people suffering from leprosy.

Mother Teresa had for some time been receiving requests for help from the large leprosy colonies around Calcutta, where thousands of people desperately needed medicines. At this time, there were about 30,000 leprosy patients in Calcutta. These patients found it hard to come to Mother Teresa's Homes for help. They did not have the money to travel in public transport, and they were too unwell to walk such long distances. When Mother Teresa saw that they could not come to her, she decided that she would go to them.

The first problem was how to reach all these areas. Then a solution presented itself. In 1956, she had been donated a van. She used this as a mobile clinic, travelling to various parts of the city to give free medical treatment to women and children, who found it hard to go to the hospitals and who were reluctant to be examined by male doctors. Mother Teresa decided to take the mobile clinic to the leprosy settlements.

In September 1957, Mother Teresa's Mobile Leprosy Clinic was inaugurated by Archbishop Perier of Calcutta. This van began to visit four large slums where people needed treatment—at Howrah, Tiljala, Dhapa and Motijhil—every week. A doctor with specialized training, along with three Sisters to nurse leprosy patients, began to make these visits. The van would be packed with medicines and food. Within a year, the mobile van was visiting four more areas as well.

The first leprosy centre that Mother Teresa set up was at Titagarh, a town a little outside Calcutta, in 1958. Before the centre was created, this area comprised of slums located on either side of a railway line, away from the main town, next to a swamp full of snakes. The slum people had no option but to live there, virtually like prisoners, as the town people would not allow leprosy patients to come near the town. They could not get any jobs, and it was very difficult for them to find food and water. No doctor or hospital would treat them.

Mother Teresa decided that she would open a leprosy centre right there, where these miserable people were living. This became the Gandhiji Prem Niwas Leprosy Centre. She handed over the responsibility for running this Home to the Brothers. Over the years, this Home has grown. The leprosy patients do everything there—from growing their own food, to constructing new buildings. They had to learn to be self-reliant because no one else would come near them to carry out any such functions. Even the saris worn by the Sisters are woven by the leprosy-affected patients who live there. This Home was very dear to Mother Teresa's heart. She was immensely proud of her leprosy people.

I visited the Gandhiji Prem Niwas in 2001 with Brother Vinod from the Missionaries of Charity in Calcutta. The centre was spread over seven and a half acres. Brother Vinod told me that the area under construction kept growing. The most recent project was housing for the leprosy patients. While they were being treated in the hospital here, they had also been allowed to make rooms for themselves where they could live with their families.

Brother Vinod showed me around. He took me to the rehabilitation section, which stood separate from the main building. Leprosy patients who were on the road to recovery, and able to carry on with normal daily activities, worked there. Rehabilitation was very important to Mother Teresa—once patients recovered, they had to go back to living normal lives again. If they were not yet ready to go back to mainstream society, at least they could live normal lives here, with their own people. Gradually, as they lived and worked here, their sense of self-worth returned and they were ready to face the world.

We went to the sheds where rows and rows of weavers were busy at their looms. Apart from saris for the Sisters, other articles needed by the Missionaries of Charity, such as dusters, napkins, bandages, curtains and bed covers were being woven. They worked at furious speed; their hands and feet flying. Those workers who had lost their feet to the disease were working the looms with their hands. Those who had lost their hands were working with their feet! They did not focus on what they had lost. Instead, they were making the most of what they had left.

Further down the long rectangular hall, workers were collecting the woven cloths. Bundles of different-coloured threads—yellows and blues and greens and mauves—made the place cheerful.

Many patients came up and greeted Brother Vinod, who seemed to know everyone by name and made affectionate enquiries. We moved on to a long line of low buildings attached to the sheds.

In one room, there was a group of teenagers working: girls sewing, and boys making canvas rucksacks. In the carpentry section, crutches were being made for patients. Outside, along the length of the building, there were lush patches of flowering plants and vegetables.

We walked by two large, clean fish tanks that supplied fish for the community twice a week. The patients had painstakingly cleared the snake-infested swamps to build these tanks in their place. I saw a bunch of boys jump into one of the tanks to swim. They had found a good way to cool off in the heat of that summer morning. In the animal husbandry section, there were pigs, chickens and other animals, kept in impeccably clean surroundings.

Further on, there was a large kitchen where all the food was cooked. We also visited a prosthetic unit, where artificial limbs for the patients were being made. On the wall were photographs of many patients, smiling into the camera. They had all been fitted with an artificial arm or leg. There was even a photograph of a Sister who had lost her leg in an accident.

At the hospital, I was taken to the separate wards for men and women. Everyone lifted their hands and said 'namaskar' to both of us. The wards, like the rest of the centre, were scrupulously clean.

The Brothers had helped to make houses for the leprosy patients to live with their families. Housing was a significant part of rehabilitation for those cured. The Brothers had been providing housing for people not just at Titagarh, but in other states as well. When I visited Titagarh, the Brothers had already built housing in West Bengal, Bihar, Orissa and Jharkand. But their aim was not just to provide housing. Wherever possible, houses were being built in 'normal' settlements or villages near the leprosy centres so that cured inmates could be eased back into the society.

As we went past the living quarters at Titagarh, there were women cooking their meals on stoves, children running around, and clothes drying in the sun. It was a normal domestic atmosphere.

In the main building, I was shown a new surgery department and new wards. Specialists and surgeons from various parts of India and abroad come as volunteers to treat the patients. They carry out reconstructive surgery to repair the affected arms, legs and other body parts of patients wherever possible. A medical department had also been opened for patients from the nearby villages to get free medical treatment. There was an eye doctor, a dentist, a homeopath, a gynaecologist and a dermatologist, who came regularly. A lot of people came several times a week to get treated for common ailments and some minor surgery.

There are today far fewer leprosy patients in India. Public awareness has made a lot of difference, at least in the cities. There are still a lot of patients in poor villages across India, but the numbers are slowly declining. The Missionaries of Charity continues to find as many cases as possible among the poor and treat them.

'I WILL DIE LIKE AN ANGEL'

Nirmal Hriday is situated in Kalighat in Calcutta. It was set up by Mother Teresa on 22 August 1952. Located next to the famous Kali temple, this is the Home that Mother Teresa set up to take care of poor people who were sick and dying.

Long before Mother Teresa set up her home at Kalighat, she was walking along a road one day, accompanied by one of the Sisters, when they saw something lying on the sidewalk. Mother Teresa thought it was a bundle of rags. When she went closer, she found to her horror that it was a middle-aged woman, who was nearly unconscious. Half her face had been eaten away by rats and ants. Mother Teresa and the Sister rushed the woman to a nearby hospital. But the hospital refused to admit the dying woman, saying that they had no free bed. Mother asked them where she should take the woman. They told her to take the woman and leave her on the road where they had found her. But Mother Teresa refused to leave the hospital and insisted they find a bed for her. Finally, realizing that Mother Teresa was a very stubborn woman, the hospital gave the woman a mattress on the floor. But it had taken too long and the woman died a few hours later, all alone and unwanted.

In the course of her work with the poor on the streets and in the slums of Calcutta, Mother Teresa had seen many heartrending sights. But she was always desolate when she found a poor person dying alone on the streets every now and then. Some were clearly so poor that they died of starvation, others from untreated illness. In their final moments, not only were they ill and suffering, but they were also completely alone. Out on the dirty streets of a crowded city, there was no one by their side to comfort them as they breathed their last.

Initially, when Mother Teresa found such people, she would take them to hospitals. But she found that most hospitals would not admit them. Most public hospitals were already very crowded with an inadequate number of beds and other facilities. When the doctors and nurses saw that the patient was on the verge of death, they did not wish to admit him or her. They argued that to do so would be to deprive someone else, who could recover, of a bed.

Mother Teresa realized that she had to do something. She could not let people simply die on the streets. Eventually, she decided to set up a shelter where she could bring the sick and dying from the streets, so she herself could take care of them. She could give them at least a comfortable place to stay, food and medicines. If treatment and recovery was possible at the Home, she could ensure that. But for those who were beyond that, the least she could do was give those who had suffered so much in life, dignity and ease in their last days.

Mother Teresa met some officials in the Calcutta municipality, and told them what she needed and why. She was sure, in her heart, that they would not turn down her request. Her wish was granted. The area that was given to her was two halls adjoining the Kali temple. This was the beginning of Nirmal Hriday.

But it was not all smooth sailing. Some people in the Kalighat area started spreading rumours that all the people who died at Nirmal Hriday, including the Hindus, were given a Christian burial. For the Hindus, this was a shocking matter. These rumours reached the ears of the municipal authorities and the officers there decided to investigate. The chief medical officer of the municipality, Dr Ahmad, accompanied by a police officer, paid an unannounced visit to Nirmal Hriday.

As the men entered the hall, they saw Mother Teresa bent over a man lying on a bed. She was so focused on her task that she did not notice them. The man she was tending had a huge, gaping wound where his face should have been. Maggots had eaten up his face and she was gently pulling the maggots out of his raw flesh. The stench was awful. But to Mother Teresa, all that mattered was helping the poor man in his agony. She told the man, 'You say a prayer in your religion, and I will say a prayer as I know it. Together we will say this prayer and it will be something beautiful for God.'

When Mother Teresa finally spotted the two visitors, she offered to show them the work in the Home. But the police officer was moved to tears by what he had just seen in action. He needed no further proof. In reply to her offer, he simply said, 'There is no need, Mother.'

When the officer went outside, a crowd had gathered—mainly trouble-makers who hoped to see Mother Teresa evicted. The officer said, 'Yes, I will send this woman away, but only after you have persuaded your mothers and sisters to come here to do the work that she is doing. This woman is a saint.'

Even after this, the hostility towards Mother Teresa did not come to an end. Some Hindus were upset that there was a place for the sick and dying people so near their holy temple, that a place for Hindu pilgrims was run by a Christian nun. Some suspected that Mother Teresa was trying to convert people to Christianity.

This was an accusation that Mother Teresa had to face many

times. Prejudice and religious bigotry made people unable to realize that Mother Teresa was doing her work for the love of God and poor people, and she did not care about the religion of those she helped. Asked if she was converting people to her religion, she once said, 'I do convert. I convert you to be a better Hindu, a better Catholic, a better Muslim, or Jain or Buddhist. I would like to help you find God. When you find Him, it is up to you to do what you want with Him.'

The cessation of hostility about Nirmal Hriday came about in an unexpected manner. There was a young priest working at the Kali temple who fell gravely ill. He was diagnosed to be in an advanced stage of tuberculosis. No hospital was willing to admit him because he was too ill to be cured, and they did not want to waste a hospital bed. There was no one else willing to take in the sick man. Finally, he was brought to Nirmal Hriday.

Mother Teresa nursed the priest. Initially, the man was angry and humiliated at being taken care of by her. But Mother Teresa took no notice of his anger. She was only interested in healing and comforting him. Gradually, the man began to calm down. He died subsequently, but he died in peace.

Meanwhile, the other priests of the temple did not fail to notice the love and care that their colleague had been given at Nirmal Hriday. They also realized that he was cremated according to Hindu rites, and not given a Christian burial that they believed all those died at Nirmal Hriday received.

After this incident, the discontent finally died down. People began to understand just how extraordinary Mother Teresa and the Missionaries of Charity were. They reached out to the poorest of the poor, the starving, sick and dying people all over the city and not only took care of their physical needs, but also gave them love and comfort. They also realized that Mother Teresa and her Sisters lived in a state of poverty that was little better than the people they served. Yes, they were fed and clothed better and lived in homes, but they had no money and no possessions, just like the poor. Their work was carried out with complete humility. Another fact that people became aware of was that people who died were given last rites according to their own religion.

Sometimes, Mother Teresa and her Sisters would bring dying people, who they found lying on the streets as they went on their daily rounds of the city, to Nirmal Hriday. Gradually, people began to make their own way to Nirmal Hriday. With great effort, they would drag themselves to the entrance and then collapse into a Sister's arms.

Whoever came to Nirmal Hriday in need of succour was immediately given a clean bed to lie on. A bath would follow, with warm, nutritious food and medical treatment. Mother Teresa and her Sisters would investigate what the problem with each person was. Often, they were in the last stages of a disease for which no further treatment was possible. Sometimes, to their joy, they would find that someone could be cured. They would give that person whatever medicine was required. The health facilities here were basic, but it was not Mother Teresa's intention to make Nirmal Hriday a hospital.

Mother Teresa could not take away the suffering these poor people had been through in their lives, but she could offer them love and respect as they lay dying. When people came to Nirmal Hriday, she would do her best to save them. If they were too ill to be saved, then Mother Teresa did her best to make them feel loved and cared for. For Mother Teresa, it was very important that when someone was dying, he or she should die peacefully, feeling loved and wanted. She understood that to die alone, feeling unloved and uncared for, was the worst kind of death for any human being. Mother Teresa and her Sisters would take care of the inmates and hold them tenderly as they died, telling them that they were loved and safe. They prayed for them, and sometimes the patient also prayed.

One day, Mother Teresa and her Sisters found a man lying in an open drain. His whole body, except for his face, was covered with wounds. They brought him to Nirmal Hriday, where they had just enough time to bathe him and put him to bed. He died soon after that. But before he died he said, 'I have lived like an animal in the street but I will die like an angel, loved and cared for.' He died with a smile on his face. There was no fear or bitterness, only an acceptance of death.

For Mother Teresa, death was 'going home to God'. She helped the dying to understand that death was not to be feared. They were simply going back to God, just as they had once come from God.

Mother Teresa was often amazed at the generosity of the poor. For instance, sometimes they would run out of beds at Nirmal Hriday. Just when Mother Teresa or the Sisters would try to figure out how to accommodate the new person who had been brought in, one of the inmates would offer his or her own bed. They would see that the newcomer was suffering even more than them and they would willingly give up the comfort of their beds.

Mother Teresa was also amazed at the courage of the poor. They had the ability to tolerate pain without a cry or a grumble. This she experienced again and again, not just with people who were dying, but with all kinds of poor people—she saw little children bravely enduring whatever physical or mental agony they were going through and people stoically bearing terrible misfortunes or disease. It was these qualities among the people she worked with that made Mother Teresa admire them so much. She also understood that it was suffering that had taught them to be so brave.

Before my first visit to Nirmal Hriday, many years ago, I was sure that a place where poor people lay sick and dying would be a depressing, even scary place. When I walked into Nirmal Hriday, I was met with the sight of a large hall with row upon row of beds, each one occupied. What amazed me initially was how clean the place was. The floors were freshly scrubbed. To one side, there was a reception area with a couple of desks. From the high windows that ran along the length of the hall, sunlight streamed in gently. The atmosphere was quiet and serene.

All around me lay thin, skeletal figures, some with wounds, or with body parts eaten up by maggots, or limbs full of sores. I did not dare go near them, and did not have the courage to look at their faces.

I focused my attention on the Sisters instead. They were moving from patient to patient, tending to them. I went and stood in one corner. I did not want to be in their way.

This hall was the men's section. Apart from the several Sisters who lived and worked here, there was a group of Brothers of the Missionaries of Charity who had come to help the Sisters, as they often did. There was also a large group of volunteers, many non-Indian—students, housewives, carpenters and mechanics, lawyers and doctors, businessmen, politicians, the rich and wealthy of Europe, North America and the Far East. They were doing the most humble of tasks—scrubbing floors, clearing bedpans, changing urine-soaked clothes and washing dirty dishes with ash. My father's story came to my mind: one day when he was working at Nirmal Hriday, he met a middle-aged American who was down on his knees, scrubbing the floor. He turned out to be a US Senator.

The volunteers were all remarkable in their own ways. Some struggled to earn a living in their own country. They would work very hard, save as much money as possible, and then buy a ticket to come and work with the poorest people at Kalighat and in Mother Teresa's other Homes! Some were rich and famous, but would work with equal dedication. There was no difference between anyone who visited—everyone was equal and everyone had just one aim: to do something to help the poor.

Near me, a man lay with his eyes closed, barely aware of the activity around him. He was thin as a skeleton. An intravenous drip was attached to his arm. Two tall, burly European men were changing his soiled clothes. A middle-aged Indian woman sat by the bed, waving a small hand fan to keep the flies away from his face. The expression on the man's face was serene. He did not seem at all scared to die.

It was lunchtime. The Sisters brought in food—warm rice, dal and vegetables. The piled plates were taken to the inmates. Many were too weak to feed themselves and the volunteers fed them.

As the volunteers and Sisters began to carry the plates into the adjoining hall—the women's section—I decided to help. I was feeling rather foolish watching everyone else work so hard. I approached one of the Sisters and she directed me to distribute the plates of food. With my heart thudding hard, I walked into the women's section.

Now I could not avoid looking at the patients. Every face was so thin and sickly, the bodies so weak that it hurt to look at them. The pain that all these men and women were suffering went straight into my heart. It was hard to look death in the eye. What can you say to a stranger who you know is dying? What consolation can you possibly offer them?

As I handed a plate to the frail woman on the first bed, she suddenly smiled at me, as if to say, 'Thank you.' Her whole face was transformed as she smiled. I could not help but smile back. Her smile deepened.

Feeling a little better, I moved on. Several women folded their hands and said 'namaskar' as I handed them their plates. One gestured to me to sit beside her. She looked about sixty, but she could have been much younger. I sat down beside her, not knowing what to say. She took my hand in hers and began to mutter to me in Bengali. I knew about three words of Bengali and tried to bring them into the conversation, hoping to establish some communication with her. She burst out laughing at my attempts. I started laughing as well.

Although we did not get very far with our dialogue, I began to see that the words did not matter, because there are so many other ways to communicate. The touch of my hand upon hers, my presence next to her, my concern for her . . . these were the things that she seemed to need. That is when I really understood how lonely these people were. They were sick and dying, with no family or friends around. Whenever I was ill, I always had my parents to look after me, friends who would call or visit.

I knew what had inspired Mother Teresa to set up Nirmal Hriday, but being here, I began to experience the power of Mother Teresa's love. And I understood why so many people came here. Though there are many organizations in the world that help the poor, what sets Mother Teresa and her Sisters apart is the fact that they give the poor much more than physical care and comfort. They did provide those as well—shelter, food, clothing and medical treatment—but they gave something much more than even that, something no one can do without. They gave love.

Many of the people who came to Nirmal Hriday had been abandoned by their families. Their families felt they had become a burden on them, perhaps because they were too old or too sick, and did not want the trouble of looking after them. Some were young people who had lost their entire families. Often, it was more than physical suffering that was killing these people. It was the terrible loneliness, the feeling of being totally unwanted that hurt more than anything else.

The woman was still holding my hand tightly. I squeezed it and then slowly released it. She smiled. It made her face glow with joy. She had asked me for so little: just a few minutes of my time, a little bit of love and compassion.

As I moved from bed to bed, I no longer felt scared or awkward. And I began to see beyond the sick and sad bodies. In the eyes of many of the women, I did not see fear, but a quiet acceptance of their situation.

Every now and then someone would ask me to sit by her bed and talk, or ask for her pillow to be adjusted, or for a drink of water. One woman kept repeating that her daughter was coming to take her home. I was very happy to hear that, until a Sister who was passing by whispered to me that this woman had been waiting for years for her daughter to come. No one believed that her daughter would ever come here for her, but in her grief, this woman was unable to accept that her daughter had abandoned her.

The woman in the last bed asked me to empty her bedpan. I had never done anything like this before. Unable to refuse her request, I gingerly picked up the bedpan and took it to the nearby toilet. I washed it clean and then brought it back to her. Instead of feeling disgusted at what I had just done, I was pleased that she had given me a chance to help her.

I recalled a story I had heard. Mother Teresa had once found a woman in a garbage dump. She had high fever and was delirious. Mother took her to Nirmal Hriday, and later asked her how she came to be in the dump. The woman said that her son had left her there. That is when Mother Teresa realized that what was killing this woman was not her illness, but a broken heart.

She could not believe that her own son had abandoned her. Mother Teresa guessed that this woman did not have much longer to live, and asked her to forgive her son. The woman refused at first. But Mother Teresa knew that until this woman forgave her son, her heart would not mend and she would not be able to die in peace. It took a long time for Mother Teresa to persuade this woman, but finally, she forgave her son. The pain in her heart eased, and she felt at peace with herself. She gave Mother Teresa a sweet, loving smile, and said, 'Thank you.' Then she died. Mother Teresa later said that this was one of the most beautiful smiles she ever received.

I wanted to talk to Sister Georgina, the most senior Sister at Nirmal Hriday. She was so busy taking care of the patients, giving the volunteers instructions, making sure everyone had had their lunch and listening to a patient's complaints that I did not think she would manage to find even a moment to talk to me. But as with all the Sisters, she made the time. She told me proudly that that year was the fiftieth anniversary of the setting up of Nirmal Hriday. In these years, they had looked after over one lakh people, several thousands of whom had recovered and returned to their lives on the streets of Calcutta. I asked hesitantly if people still came, given that Mother Teresa was not there any more. Sister Georgina said that more people were coming now than ever before. I was curious to know why. She laughed and said with a twinkle in her eye, 'Well, now that Mother is in Heaven, she finds it much easier to send [the sick people] right to our door!'

I had come to Nirmal Hriday feeling fear, even anticipating horror, because I thought that death was something to be frightened of. But despite the pain and suffering, Nirmal Hriday was so full of love and peace! That is how I learnt that death can, and should be, full of love, compassion and dignity.

Every time I have gone to Calcutta since that first visit, I have returned to Nirmal Hriday. The special atmosphere in this Home seemed a reflection of the love and light Mother Teresa had herself. Although Mother Teresa is no longer physically there, I feel her spirit very strongly. The special quality of love and peace that pervades this Home has not changed.

Many volunteers and visitors keep returning to work or visit. They too feel the same peace here. But eventually volunteers from outside the city have to return to their own homes, and volunteers from Calcutta have to go back to their own lives. The work carries on because of the Sisters who run Nirmal Hriday, who spend every day tending to the ill and dying.

It is very hard to be surrounded by so much suffering and the constant presence of death, but the Sisters love working at Nirmal Hriday. Many Sisters try to get a posting to this Home. For Mother Teresa herself, this Home was particularly special. She had said, 'You feel the presence of God there, and they [the poor] feel the love they get.'*

---

* Gonzalez-Balado and Playfoot, ed., *My Life for the Poor: Mother Teresa of Calcutta.*

THE WORK CONTINUES

For the first ten years, the Missionaries of Charity worked only in Calcutta. Church law did not allow an organization to open Homes outside the diocese for the first ten years. The first Home outside Calcutta was finally opened in Ranchi in 1960. The next one was opened in Delhi and inaugurated by Prime Minister Jawaharlal Nehru. By the end of the 1960s, the number of Homes in India had grown to twenty-five. The first Home abroad was set up in Venezuela in 1965. This was followed by one in Rome in 1968 and one in Australia in 1969. Homes were set up in quick succession in other parts of the world.

As the Missionaries of Charity spread all over the world, Mother Teresa began to travel a lot. She spent about six months every year travelling to see the work her Sisters were doing, to inspect places where there was a proposal to set up a new Home and to establish them. She wanted to see for herself what the particular needs of poor people were in a particular place, and work out how her organization could best help.

Mother Teresa did not waste too much time in planning. She addressed a need where she saw it. For instance, where she saw many poor old people on the streets of a city, there she decided to set up a Home for the elderly. Elsewhere, when she discovered people suffering from leprosy, she worked to set up a Home for them. When AIDS became a problem in some city, she set up a shelter for AIDS patients there. She always started with whatever resources she could muster up, never making grandiose plans. She was invariably very practical in her work and approach.

Mother Teresa was filled with joy each time the decision to set up a new Home was taken. She saw this as an opportunity for more and more poor people to receive love and care. She was willing to go wherever God sent her, so that she could help people.

But setting up the infrastructure for a new Home, and establishing it so that it could sustain itself cost a lot of money. Mother Teresa made it a rule that she would accept donations of money, food, clothing and other things only from private individuals or organizations. She refused to take money from the Church or from the government of any country. She felt that if she took money from the Church or any government, she would be obliged to keep meticulous accounts of how the money was spent to submit to the donors. She could ill afford to spare one of her Sisters for the task. Each Sister who got involved in such tasks meant that a poor person somewhere was being deprived of a Sister's much-needed care and service. She only accepted donations that came without any conditions attached. She was also comfortable with accepting donations in kind. Many of her Homes all over the world are greatly dependent on such donations.

There were often times when in some Home or the other, the Sisters would run out of food. The Sisters were not concerned about going hungry themselves. What worried them was how they would feed their inmates, or what food they would take to the poor outside on the streets. With no options left, all they could do was pray for help. And invariably, some food would miraculously arrive suddenly from a kind donor!

As the Missionaries of Charity developed, different kinds of programmes were put in place. One important programme was the medical programme, which included Homes for the sick and dying, the mentally and physically challenged, the leprosy affected, tuberculosis patients, children and old people, and in later years, those suffering from AIDS. Homes were also set up for alcoholics and drug addicts.

Another important segment of the work done by the Missionaries of Charity was the educational programme. Classes were organized in deprived localities. Poor children were placed in schools. Young people were trained in different vocational skills so that they were in a position to earn their own living.

As part of the social programmes of the organization, day crèches were set up for children whose mothers needed to go out and work. Night shelters were set up for poor people so that they had a safe place to rest and sleep.

As time went by, Mother Teresa began to receive help from people all over the world. They came to offer their help as volunteers and to work in the Homes along with the Sisters. This was usually in the Homes that the Missionaries of Charity had set up in their own cities, but in increasing numbers people also travelled to India to work in the Homes.

Over the years, there were many people who wanted to visit Calcutta and Motherhouse. They wanted to meet the woman who had become an icon of love and peace all over the world. And they wanted to offer their services in her Homes there, even if it was for a brief while.

It became a common sight to find volunteers working in Missionaries of Charity Homes in India as well as abroad. Though the Sisters do the bulk of the work, volunteers, help in washing, feeding, dispensing medicines and other small tasks. They also offer companionship to the inmates. This carries on even today, much after Mother Teresa's death. Volunteers continue to be very important to the work, making a difference with their support, both to the Sisters as well as the inmates. Working in Mother Teresa's Homes gives volunteers a sense of being a part of the Missionaries of Charity family.

Donations were almost always used up instantly, because there was always a need in some Home or the other for food, medicines and other supplies. Mother Teresa did not believe in saving money or hoarding it. She always said that whenever there was need for it, God would provide.

Though some of the donations were huge, many were small. A poor person might donate a few rupees. For Mother Teresa, who used to say, 'Give until it hurts,' such a donation meant a lot. To give when one barely has enough for one's own needs is to be truly generous. When Mother Teresa was asked why she took money from people who could ill afford to give, she explained that for that poor person, giving her a gift of a few rupees was a very big thing. It was a big sacrifice and she could see with how much love that person had come to her bearing his or her gift. If she turned down that gift of love, it would break that giver's heart.

People also gave donations of food, clothes, toiletries, medicines and many other things—even old newspapers and boxes, wool, plastic sheets and junk materials. Mother Teresa and the Sisters found a use for everything. No gift or donation was too small in their eyes.

But there were certain gifts that Mother Teresa refused, such as washing machines, refrigerators and other expensive items. The Sisters and Brothers lived very austerely, and Mother Teresa had always believed that their lives should be as simple as the people they served. They did not wish for comforts.

However, what would be useful for her work, she accepted

gratefully. For example, in both India and abroad, people donated houses to her that she gladly used to set up Homes for the needy.

People from all walks of life wanted to help Mother Teresa. This included many wealthy and influential people in India and abroad. People in the government helped her with administrative work: such as permissions, visas and passports. She needed help for electricity problems in one Home or the urgent need to deliver medicines to another. There were always friends and well-wishers who would step in to sort out such problems. She had no hesitation in asking for help, and she was rarely refused. Her friends included prime ministers, royalty, politicians and heads of business families, who were all eager to assist her whenever she asked. She became a spiritual guide for many people, rich and poor, who came to her for advice and support, be it in personal matters or professional matters.

This could also be for something completely trivial. When studying for school or college examinations, my sister and I would call up Mother Teresa in Calcutta to ask for her blessings. She would always tell us that we would do well and that she would pray for us. The next morning, on the blackboard outside the chapel at Motherhouse, a note would be written, asking everyone to pray for both of us. Our names were written there. In fact, each time I visited Motherhouse, I would see such notices scribbled on the blackboard, asking all the Sisters to pray for such and such person. Mother Teresa never laughed at our small requests, but took them seriously. When my sister was in college, she was going through some problem with her boyfriend. My father suggested she talk to Mother Teresa. So my sister telephoned Mother Teresa to tell her briefly about her problem. Mother Teresa offered to pray for her. I am sure Mother Teresa and her Sisters were amused about this particular problem about boyfriends.

In 1973, Mother Teresa was sixty-three. She felt old and tired, and often fell ill. She developed a heart problem that stayed with her for the rest of her life. Over the next decade, she tried several times to step down as the head of the organization and to have another Sister appointed in her place. But the Sisters would not accept this decision. Touched by their devotion and love, Mother Teresa reluctantly agreed to stay on each time.

In 1989, the cardiac problems became more serious and she had to have a pacemaker installed. This time, she approached the Vatican in Rome asking for permission to step down. She wanted the Missionaries of Charity to have an election to vote for a new head. Although the Vatican granted her the permission to have the general election, the Sisters refused to change their mind.

Mother Teresa finally accepted this decision. As always, she was ready to accept God's will, and He clearly wanted her to continue the work she was doing.

Perhaps it was inevitable that the work Mother Teresa and her organization were doing would earn her recognition. But she never cared for fame and recognition. Hers was a work of love. When awards came, she always received them in the name of God and as acknowledgement for the people she worked with. They meant nothing to her personally, but they represented recognition for the poor.

The first major award that she received was the Padma Shri in 1962, which was conferred at the Rashtrapati Bhawan. A few months later, she won the Ramon Magsasay Award from the Philippines. This award, as it turned out, was of great significance to Mother Teresa. She had been wanting to set up a Home for people suffering from leprosy in Agra. But she found that she did not have the funds. She informed her Sisters of this problem. The very same day, she was suddenly told of this award and the

Rs 50,000 that came with it! Her prayers had been answered once again.

In 1979, Mother Teresa was awarded the Nobel Prize for Peace. Accompanied by Sister Agnes and Sister Gertrude, her very first postulants, Mother Teresa travelled to Oslo, Norway, for the presentation ceremony on 10 December. In the presence of the King of Norway and dignitaries and media from around the world, Mother Teresa received the award.

The Nobel Peace Prize ensured that people over the world who had previously not heard of the work she was doing now knew about it. She was acknowledged as a symbol of love and peace in the world.

Other awards followed, including the Order of Merit from Queen Elizabeth II of Great Britain, the highest decoration given in that country. This was awarded in 1983, and the Queen personally conferred the award when she visited Delhi a short while later.

Some of the most highly esteemed universities in the world such as Harvard and Cambridge conferred honorary doctorates upon Mother Teresa. She had never even been to college! Mother Teresa's photographs were visible everywhere, from the covers of international magazines to the postage stamps of India and Sweden. But through all this acclaim and recognition, her focus never wavered from working with the poor and destitute of the world.

'GOING HOME TO GOD'

In the late 1990s, as Mother Teresa grew more tired and ill, she insisted on having a successor elected.

An election was finally held and a new successor was found on 13 March 1997. Sister Nirmala, one of Mother Teresa's most senior Sisters, would head the organization henceforth. Mother Teresa knew that her successor would carry out her responsibilities with integrity and love. She accompanied Sister Nirmala to the Vatican to meet Pope John Paul II and to take his blessings. However, Sister Nirmala refused to be called 'Mother' as befitted the head of the organization. For the Missionaries of Charity, there would always be only one 'Mother'.

Over the next few months, Mother Teresa's health began to deteriorate. On the night of 3 September, she was suddenly taken ill. She was too unwell to attend Mass the next day, though it was something she would never miss. Through the day, her Sisters, including Sister Gertrude and Sister Nirmala, took turns being with her.

On 5 September, Mother Teresa made an immense effort to get out of bed. She attended Mass, and spent the day meeting visitors and talking to the Sisters and Brothers. By evening she was exhausted and had to return to bed. She spent the next few hours in unbearable agony.

'Pope John Paul blesses Mother Teresa' *by Katyayani Sinha*

'Mother Teresa has left the world' *by Katyayani Sinha*

At about 8 p.m., Mother Teresa developed a breathing problem and was unable to breathe on her own. The Sisters hurriedly put an oxygen mask on her mouth. Just then, the electricity went off, a very rare occurrence. It came back after four minutes, but these had been critical minutes. Mother Teresa was gasping for breath.

A few minutes later, she took her last breath and went home to God.

The entire city went into mourning. The beloved mother of the poor had gone. The next day, her body was taken to St. Thomas's Church, where she lay in state under the Indian national flag for the next six days. Hundreds of thousands of people from Calcutta as well as other parts of the country and world, came to pay their respects to Mother Teresa. People came with flowers and wreaths and prayers, children with hymns.

On 13 September, her body was placed in a gun carriage—the same one used for the funerals of Gandhiji and Pandit Jawaharlal Nehru—and taken to Eden Gardens, Calcutta's largest stadium. Her funeral was attended by the then president, K.R. Narayanan and Prime Minister I.K. Gujral. Presidents, prime ministers and emissaries of thirty-six countries were also present. Delegates included Hillary Clinton, Queen Noor of Jordan, Queen Sophia of Spain and Queen Fabiola of Belgium, and several cardinals from the Vatican. The Sisters and Brothers of the Missionaries of Charity were in attendance, along with volunteers and other workers.

Hymns were sung in English, Hindi and Bengali by the Sisters. People from different religious groups from various parts of India presented readings from their sacred texts.

As the procession left the stadium and made its way along the streets to Motherhouse, thousands and thousands of people lined up to catch a final glimpse of their 'ma'. Tears were pouring down countless faces. The sense of loss was overwhelming.

Mother Teresa had chosen her own home as her final abode and had asked to be buried in the large hall on the ground floor, directly below the chapel.

As the coffin was lowered gently into its final resting place, the Sisters sang hymns. Outside, bugles sounded and army officers fired a gun salute.

Mother Teresa's tombstone was simple. On it were the words, 'Love one another as I have loved you.'

THE MAKING OF A SAINT

For innumerable people the world over, Mother Teresa had long been a living saint. But they wanted her to be formally recognized as a saint, like others granted that status by the Catholic Church.

The power to declare someone a saint in the Catholic Church rests with the Pope and other senior officials in the Vatican. There are several stages in this process, which can take many years to complete. The process can begin only five years after the death of the person who is a candidate for canonization. The bishop of the diocese in which this person dies is responsible for beginning the investigation. The bishop forms a diocesan tribunal, and witnesses are called to recount examples of when this person showed behaviour and character that befits a saint. Documents are gathered and sent to the Congregation for the Causes of Saints, which is located in the Vatican. At this point, the person is entitled to the title of Servant of God.

In the Congregation, various theologians, cardinals and bishops examine the documentation. If they believe that the person deserves to be beatified, they pass on their recommendations to the Holy Father.

For the Pope to beatify a person, there must be some evidence of a miracle attributed to the Servant of God. This miracle must be proved through canonical investigation. When this is proven, the Holy Father grants the Servant of God the title of Blessed.

For canonization, another miracle is needed, attributed to the intercession of the Blessed and having occurred after the beatification. Once this is affirmed, the person is canonized, or can be publicly worshipped in any Christian church. After canonization, the Blessed acquires the title of Saint.

In October 1997, the Archbishop Henry D'Souza of Calcutta formally wrote to the Vatican, asking for permission to start the enquiry into Mother Teresa, the first stage in the canonization process, without waiting for the regulation five years. Pope John Paul II, who was familiar with Mother Teresa's work, granted special permission to start the enquiry well before the prescribed time period was over. This was the first time that a such special dispensation had been granted.

The formal enquiry started in July 1999. The Missionaries of Charity had to submit many documents about Mother Teresa to the diocesan tribunal. The report of the tribunal was sent to the Congregation for the Causes of Saints. A long period of research followed.

After this, in order for Mother Teresa to be beatified, they needed proof of a miracle, of her having healed someone, instantaneously and permanently, without depending on any scientific or other kind of help.

For most people, this seemed beside the point. Mother Teresa had created miracles every day, in the lives that she touched and transformed, in the light that she brought into dark lives, in the hearts that she mended and the bodies that she tended to.

However, the Church needed formal evidence. People began to come forward to share stories of their interactions with Mother Teresa and how she had changed their lives. The Missionaries of Charity was inundated with letters and phone calls. The search continued for tangible proof of such a miracle that the Church would be ready to accept.

Monica Besra, from a village called Dakshin Dinajpur in West Bengal, said that Mother Teresa had cured her of a tumour in her stomach and healed her completely. Monica had been ill since November 1997. It started with minor problems such as nausea and fever, but kept getting worse. She went to many doctors, but no one seemed to be able to diagnose the problem, let alone cure it.

After a while, Monica discovered a lump in her stomach, which developed into a tumour. Though doctors were able to identify the problem, they still did not know how to solve it. No medication seemed to work. In desperation, she sought the help of the Missionaries of Charity Sisters in a small town in West Bengal. The Sisters got her admitted to a government hospital. That did not help either.

Monica was then hospitalized in Calcutta in the summer of 1998. Her stomach was very large by now, and she was unable to take care of herself. The Sisters were her constant attendants.

A few months went by and Monica's situation only worsened. There seemed no medical solution.

Finally, the Sisters decided on a different course of action. They began to pray. One of them placed a medallion of the Virgin Mary that Mother Teresa had given her, on Monica's swollen stomach. They also asked Monica to pray to Mother Teresa's photograph.

On 5 September 1998, the first anniversary of Mother Teresa's death, Monica began praying with the Sisters. A few hours later, she looked down at her stomach to find that the swelling had disappeared. She was also feeling much better.

When she returned to the doctors for a checkup, they were unable to find the tumour they had earlier found!

The tale of Monica's miraculous cure met the conditions

required by the Vatican. This paved the way for the beatification. In December 2002, Pope John Paul II formally announced this.

The world rejoiced. Amidst great joy and celebration, Mother Teresa was beatified in the St. Peter's Basilica in the Vatican on 19 October 2003. Thousands of people travelled to Rome to witness this moving ceremony.

I had the good fortune to travel to Rome with my parents a few days before Mother Teresa's beatification. The whole city wore a festive atmosphere. It was packed to capacity; all the hotels and guest houses were full. The area around the Vatican was bedecked with flowers and flags. People waved pictures of Mother Teresa.

It was a glorious sight to see hundreds of nuns, clad in simple white saris with blue borders, walking around the Vatican. Many years earlier, Pope John Paul II had given the Missionaries of Charity a house within the precincts of the Vatican. Many of the Sisters, who had travelled there from different parts of the world, were staying at this house. Many other Christian organizations from across the world had sent their representatives to be a part of this historical event.

Before the actual ceremony of beatification, there were other ceremonies and festivities in and around the Vatican, including concerts, prayers, special Masses and a film about Mother Teresa. I remember one particular concert which was packed to capacity by visiting dignitaries, the press, and nuns and priests of different religious organizations, dressed in different robes and gowns. I felt great pride when I saw, near the stage, a large band of white and blue—the Missionaries of Charity Sisters. At some point, the Pope arrived to address the audience. He spoke about Mother Teresa with a lot of love. He and Mother Teresa had been very close. I'm told that he said he used to find it very hard to say no to her whenever she asked him for some help for the poor.

At the screening of the film on the life of Mother Teresa, the audience was smaller, but equally emotional. Many people began to cry as Mother Teresa's life unfolded on the large screen before us.

The weather during this time was cold, wet and windy. As the beatification ceremony was to be held outdoors, everyone was rather concerned. The night before the ceremony, my parents and I were taking shelter from the rain at Mother Teresa's home in the Vatican, as were a lot of Sisters. The corridor at the entrance was full of Sisters in soaking saris. As I stood shivering in my coat, sweaters and gloves, I noticed that some of the Sisters were wearing just rubber slippers and thin sweaters. Laughing and chatting with one another, they did not even seem to notice the biting cold.

I remarked to one of the Sisters that I hoped that the following day would not be rainy. She said with a twinkle in her eye, 'There are so many flowers out there. They all need to be watered, otherwise they will die by tomorrow. That is why Mother is sending rain today. Tomorrow morning, you will see, there will be bright sunshine! Mother will take care of the weather, don't worry.' I loved the spirit of the Sisters; they were always positive and cheerful, and with so much faith in Mother.

The following day dawned bright and sunny. We gathered in the courtyard of St. Peter's Basilica in the very heart of the Vatican, where there was seating for several hundred people. This is the most sacred pilgrimage for Roman Catholics the world over. We could see thousands of people gathered in the square below, as far as the eye could see. It seemed that the entire city had come to watch this ceremony.

To my growing dismay, the sun that had shone so promisingly earlier that morning was now playing hide-and-seek with the clouds. After a while, it simply disappeared. The crowds were also gazing anxiously at the sky, which was now filled with dark clouds. This was not right, I thought. But just as the ceremony was about to begin, however, the sun came out again, and in minutes there was not a cloud in the sky!

The ceremony was long and complicated, much of it conducted in Latin by a large number of priests. The Pope sat quietly in the middle. At one point, everyone burst into applause, and I realized that Mother Teresa was now formally beatified. There was a sudden movement from a balcony above our heads. A large beautiful portrait of Mother Teresa was dropped down and her beloved face smiled down at us. With the bright sunlight falling on the portrait, she was aglow with golden light. It seemed to me that she had come down to bless us.

There were more hymns and prayers that followed, sung by other nuns as well as the Missionaries of Charity Sisters before the function ended.

There is one more stage before Mother Teresa is formally declared a saint. There is another 'miracle' which has to be proved. But for those whose lives have been transformed by her, she has long been a saint.

EPILOGUE

The first time I went to Calcutta after Mother Teresa's death, I found myself wondering if the work and the spirit of the Missionaries of Charity still remained the same. I talked to many of the Sisters to find out how they felt. At Motherhouse, I asked Sister Lisa how she felt without Mother Teresa around. Sister Lisa smiled. 'Now that Mother's physical presence is not here,' she said, 'we strive even harder to follow her teachings and do the work. When parents go away and leave the children at home, the children have to take responsibility for the home. They have to work even harder to take care of it. And so, we are all working even harder than before to fulfil Mother's dream, to be faithful daughters. She was God's most perfect instrument. Our work is for God, but we will always be our Mother's daughters.'

There were few visible changes in Motherhouse. Outside the hall where Mother Teresa lay in her simple tomb, there was a life-sized bronze statue of her. It had been donated to the organization by someone. As I watched, a young girl came up and placed her head below the statue's outstretched hand, as if taking Mother Teresa's blessings! Another person arrived to touch the bronze feet. Mother Teresa's grave has now become a pilgrimage site. Sister Gertrude, who was passing by, laughed. She said, 'First they used to come and see her, now they come to see her tombstone!'

At Shishu Bhawan, I met Sister Marjorie, who was looking after the children there. As we talked about Mother Teresa, Sister Marjorie said to me, 'You know, when Mother was alive, we did not see her very often, she had so much work and so much travel. But now, in spirit, she is always here with us. I talk to her whenever I have a problem and I see how she helps, in so many ways.'

These words were echoed by Sister Rosebella, whom I met recently at Jeevan Jyoti in Delhi. She said, '[Mother] is always there. So many times when I am in a difficulty, I pray to Mother and she sends help for me. Whatever problem I am having is solved. Mother is so close to us.'

Nirmal Hriday at Kalighat remains unchanged.

The question I had wanted to answer when I came to Calcutta was whether Mother Teresa's work was continuing as it would have had she been alive. And the answer was a joyful yes. Nothing had changed. I myself could feel Mother Teresa's presence everywhere. She had inspired so many people, be they the Sisters and Brothers, volunteers or visitors who came to see her Homes and her work. That inspiration is still evident today. In the faces of the Sisters as they work with the poor, I can see reflections of the radiance that I had seen in Mother's face. Mother Teresa as a symbol of unconditional love and peace will always remain in the hearts and minds of people all over the world.

The Missionaries of Charity continues to grow. Every now and then, a new girl will arrive at Motherhouse to train as and become a nun, a process which takes several years.

At present, there are about 234 Homes in India and 490 Homes in other countries of the world. This number changes constantly. Homes are opened and shut in different places, due to political or practical reasons, depending on the need that arises in a particular place. This also determines the kind of Homes set up. For example, AIDS hospices were set up in Los Angeles and New York, and leprosy Homes in various parts of Africa. When there were famines in Ethiopia during the 1960s and 1970s, Mother Teresa set up feeding centres there. She also set up soup kitchens in London so that cold and hungry, homeless people could come into a warm, protective environment and receive hot food.

Mother Teresa saw a lot of loneliness in the West, more a 'spiritual poverty' than a physical one. So a system was worked out whereby volunteers would visit the lonely, elderly people who remained isolated in their apartments, with no family or loved ones to look after them. The volunteers provided them with company and helped in small ways around the apartment.

At present, the Missionaries of Charity is working in 131 countries. Over the decades, the Missionaries of Charity has set up Homes in countries all over the world: Africa, other parts of Asia, South America, North America, Europe (both western and eastern Europe), the Middle East, the Indian subcontinent and the Far East.

ANNEXURE

A Simple Life

Mother Teresa's life was lived very simply. There were some central beliefs on which she based her life and work. This was her special prayer:

> The fruit of Silence is Prayer.
> The fruit of Prayer is Faith.
> The fruit of Faith is Love.
> The fruit of Love is Service.
> The fruit of Service is Peace.

PRAYER

Prayer was Mother Teresa's way of reaching out to God, asking Him for strength, guidance and love. Prayer was her way of thanking God for His Love. She would ask everyone to pray to God according to whatever religion they believed in. She would pray for all human beings, especially the poor, who needed help most of all. Prayer filled Mother Teresa with joy and gave her faith.

FAITH

Mother Teresa lived her life in a complete and total surrender to God. It was her faith in God that gave her the strength to leave home and go to a new land. It was her faith that gave her the strength to go through great hardships in her life, loneliness and humiliations that she had to face, especially in her early years. It was this same faith in God that allowed her to live her dream and to believe in it wholeheartedly. Mother Teresa never gave up. She started her life with nothing but her faith. Out of that faith grew her organization. From a single nun working by herself in a Calcutta slum, it was her total and complete faith in God that led to the creation of a worldwide organization.

LOVE

Mother Teresa's work was all about love. Each decision she took was born of her complete love for God. Each poor person she reached out to, to comfort and help and heal, she did with great love for him or her. She loved every single poor person. To her, they were all part of God Himself. In each poor person, she saw the face of God, and through loving them, she was loving God. Though the poor people of the world were her special people, she loved everyone. She never judged anyone, no matter what they had done wrong. Her way was of love, peace and forgiveness. It is because her dream was a dream of love, made out of a pure heart, with love as its purpose, that Mother Teresa succeeded.

JOY

Mother Teresa believed that the only way to do the work of helping the poor, was to do it with joy. She and her Sisters were always cheerful and smiling. To do something with joy was to express gratitude to God for all the love He had given her, and for the very special task he had bestowed on her. Mother Teresa maintained that one had to go to the poor with joy and good cheer. It was useless to help the poor while looking and feeling miserable. Those who were suffering would take strength and inspiration from a smiling and happy face.

SERVICE

Mother Teresa's life was a life of service. She served God through her service to the poorest of the poor. She lived only to serve and asked for nothing in return. She wanted neither money nor recognition. To her, life was beautiful because she had been given the chance to serve others.